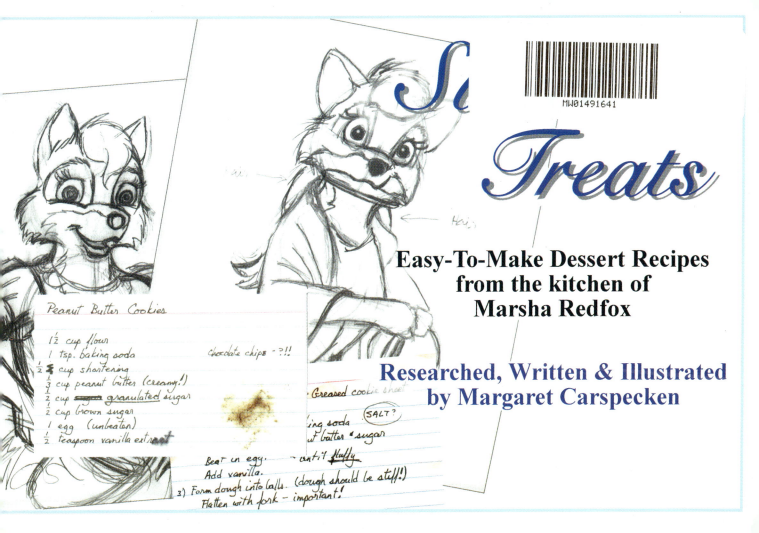

S̲ *Treats*

Easy-To-Make Dessert Recipes
from the kitchen of
Marsha Redfox

Researched, Written & Illustrated
by Margaret Carspecken

Peanut Butter Cookies

1½ cup flour
1 tsp. baking soda
½ cup shortening
⅓ cup peanut butter (creamy!)
½ cup ~~sugar~~ granulated sugar
½ cup brown sugar
1 egg (unbeaten)
½ teaspoon vanilla extract

Chocolate chips - ?!!

Greased cookie sheet

~~ing~~ soda
~~ut~~ butter + sugar
SALT?

Beat in egg. until ~~fluffy~~
Add vanilla.
3) Form dough into balls. (dough should be stiff!)
Flatten with fork - important!

R&M Creative Endeavors

For information, write:
Vision Books, P.O. Box 580009, Flushing, NY, 11358-0009.

The Vision Books World Wide Web Site address is
http://vision.nais.com

The R&M Creative Endeavours Web Site address is
http://www.ozfoxes.com

ISBN: 1-887038-02-7

Vision Books are published by Vision Entertainment,
Post Office Box 580009, Flushing, NY, 11358-0009.

PRINTED IN CANADA

VISION BOOKS

Table of Contents

Welcome . . .

...to Marsha's World, and to mine!

Marsha has been a dear and close friend for a very long time. We live in different worlds, but in many ways we are the same person. I am *very* happy to say that my life is not nearly as exciting as hers; but we enjoy swapping stories, and secrets—and recipes. I am usually left with figuring out how to make the recipes work. That's how this all started.

This cookbook is designed to let people create tasty desserts of all kinds, no matter what your level of culinary expertise might be. Desserts really aren't hard, if you are willing to practice making them a little. The nice thing about the desserts in this book is, even the failures are delicious! (And if something goes wrong, you can eat the evidence.)

A few notes and hints

• These recipes have been structured to allow for small batches wherever possible. I always find it easier to double a recipe than to halve it!

- Most ingredients used in these recipes can be found on your grocery store shelves.
- To make any recipe in this book, only basic kitchen equipment is needed. I recommend the following:

For measuring:
- Measuring spoons
- Measuring cups

For mixing and preparation:
- Mixing spoons (wooden spoons are nice!)
- Rolling pin
- Rubber spatulas
- Mixing bowls (metal or glass are best)
- Pastry cutter
- Wire whisk
- Pastry brush
- Sifter

For baking or serving:
Oven-proof casserole dish
8-inch square baking pan
9x13-inch baking pan
Pie pans
Cookie sheets

Other helpful equipment:
- An electric mixer is *very* handy for recipes using whipped egg whites. You can use a hand-cranked beater if you have strong arm muscles and are quick enough; but the electric variety is much nicer!
- A food processor or electric blender helps with recipes that use ground or finely chopped nuts. Either appliance saves enormous amounts of time and chef-energy!

Nifty Tricks and Tips

- **Sifting:** It may not be acceptable practice in fancy kitchens, but a wire whisk works nicely to "sift" flour or to combine dry ingredients. Powdered sugar and cocoa, however, should *always* be sifted with a conventional sifter.
- **Adding Eggs to Melted Ingredients:** Whenever eggs are added to hot or melted ingredients (hot milk, melted chocolate chips, etc.), be sure that the heated ingredients are sufficiently cooled so as not to cook the egg.
- **Vegetable Cooking Sprays:** These make for fast and even greasing of glass or metal pans. However, if you have

specially-coated non-stick pans, do *not* use cooking spray on them! Baked-on vegetable spray can ruin specially-coated pans.

- **Baking With Glass Baking Dishes:** Glass retains heat longer than metal, so reduce your oven temperature by 25° when using glass baking pans to prevent overbaking your dessert. I give both temperatures in most of the recipes, because this alteration is very easy to forget!

- **Butter or Margarine?** Butter makes for a richer dessert, but margarine can be substituted in any recipe that calls for butter, and the results will still be delicious. Always use margarine that comes in the stick form, however; soft tub margarines often have a higher liquid content that may affect the quality of your dessert.

- **Microwaves and Chocolate Chips:** If you use a microwave oven to melt chocolate chips, remember that the chips will hold their shape and will not *look* melted, even when they are soft and gooey. Stir the chips with a spoon to check their consistency.

- **What is Folding?** *Folding* is a method of combining ingredients where the 'fluffiness' is maintained using air bubbles. (Meringue and whipped cream are good examples of 'fluffy' ingredients.) When adding heavier ingredients to a fluffy mixture, it is important that you maintain the fluffiness. Folding is done using a rubber spatula: cut down through the ingredients with the spatula, then bring it back up, lifting the ingredients from the bottom of the bowl as you do so. Rotate the bowl and repeat this action until all the ingredients are mixed and fluffy.

- **What is Cutting?** If you try to mix butter or shortening into flour with a spoon, you will end up with a lump of floured shortening — hardly the desired result. *Cutting* involves slicing the shortening into tiny pieces and working it into the dry ingredients at the same time. This can be done with a special Pastry Cutter; or you can use two knives, slicing them sideways in a scissor-like fashion. When the shortening can no longer be identified, and the flour (or other dry ingredients) look crumbly or pebbly, the butter or shortening has been "cut in" correctly.

- **How do I beat egg whites into a meringue?** Get a head start, or distract the eggs by making them laugh... no, let's be serious. Separate the egg yolks and the egg whites while the eggs are cold. (An egg separator is useful here!) Be

continued on next page

very careful that *no* yolk gets into the egg white. Place the egg whites in a mixing bowl, preferably a glass or metal bowl; plastic mixing bowls sometimes retain a faint greasy residue which would prevent the egg whites from beating up properly.

Here's a quick walk-through:

Let the egg whites sit for about 30 minutes at room temperature. Begin beating them with an electric mixer. When the egg whites start to stand up in soft, rounded peaks when the beaters are lifted, start adding sugar — but only a little at a time, beating the sugar in thoroughly after each addition; adding all the sugar at once will cause your meringue to collapse. Continue beating until the meringue stands up in peaks that hold their shape when the beaters are lifted. (If you rub a little of the meringue between your fingers, it should feel smooth, not gritty with undissolved sugar.)

Voila! You've made a meringue!

- **<u>What can I do with leftover egg whites/yolks?</u>**
Here is a quick list of recipes that use only egg whites, or only egg yolks:

Egg Whites	Egg Yolks
Angel Food Loaf Cake	
Chocolate Puffs	Custard Sauce
Cherry-Nut Puffs	Lemon Curd
Mint Puffs	Nane Shirini
Missikiti	Sesame Cookies

If you make a dessert from column A, make one from column B at the same time. What a great excuse to make two desserts at once!

That's the basics. Have fun looking through the book, and enjoy your Sweet Treats!

Cakes and Teatime Treats

Gingerbread

Old-fashioned goodness in a cake

6 tablespoons brown sugar,
   firmly packed
6 tablespoons vegetable oil
6 tablespoons molasses
1 egg
1 cup + 2 tablespoons flour
1¼ teaspoons baking powder
¼ teaspoon baking soda
1 teaspoon ground ginger
¾ teaspoon ground cinnamon
½ teaspoon ground allspice
½ cup boiling water

Preheat the oven to 350° F. (325° if you are using a glass pan). Grease an 8-inch square baking pan and set aside.

In large mixing bowl combine the sugar, vegetable oil and molasses. Add the egg and beat well with a wooden spoon.

In a separate bowl, stir together the dry ingredients with a spoon or wire whisk. Add the dry ingredients to the sugar mixture, mixing well. Add the boiling water, stirring gently.

Pour the batter into the prepared pan, and bake for 25 minutes or until a toothpick inserted in the center comes out clean.

Apple Cake

Flavors of Autumn baked in a cake!

1 cup sugar
⅓ cup shortening, softened
1 egg
1½ cups flour, sifted
1 teaspoon soda
½ teaspoon salt
½ teaspoon ground cinnamon
½ teaspoon ground nutmeg
¼ cup milk
2 cups grated, peeled apple (about 2 large apples)
½ cup walnuts
1 teaspoon vanilla extract

TOPPING:
½ cup brown sugar, firmly packed
2 tablespoons flour
3 tablespoons butter or margarine

Preheat the oven to 350° F. (325° F. if you are using a glass pan). Grease and flour an 8-inch square baking pan and set aside.

In a large mixing bowl, cream together the sugar and shortening using a spoon or electric mixer. Add the egg and beat in.

In a separate bowl, stir together the flour with the soda, salt, cinnamon, and nutmeg. Add the dry ingredients to the creamed mixture, alternately adding milk and apples. When all the dry ingredients, the milk and the apples have been mixed into the creamed mixture, add the walnuts and vanilla extract. Mix well. Pour the batter into the greased/floured pan.

Combine the topping ingredients and sprinkle over the cake. Bake for about 30 to 35 minutes, or until a toothpick inserted in the center of cake comes out clean.

Irish Batter Muffins

1 egg, well beaten
1½ cups milk, buttermilk, or soured milk*
3 tablespoons grated orange peel
1 cup currants
2 tablespoons vegetable oil
3 cups flour
½ cup sugar
4 teaspoons baking powder
2 teaspoons ground cinnamon
1 teaspoon salt

*To make soured milk: Place 1 tablespoon lemon juice in a measuring cup and add milk to make 1½ cup of liquid. Mix, then allow to sit for about 5 minutes.

Grease 9 regular-sized muffin cups.

In a small mixing bowl, combine the egg, milk, and grated orange peel. Blend in the vegetable oil. Stir in the currants, then set the mixture aside.

In a large mixing bowl, sift together the flour, sugar, baking powder, cinnamon, and salt. Make a well in center of the dry ingredients and add the liquid mixture all at one time. Mix with a wooden spoon to moisten the dry ingredients, about 15 to 20 strokes; do not over-mix. Spoon the dough into greased muffin cups and let stand at room temperature for 20 minutes.

Preheat oven to 325° F. Bake for about 1 hour or until muffins test done. Cool and store for 12 to 24 hours before serving.

This recipe can also be baked in a loaf pan, at 300° for 90 minutes.

Irish Soda Bread

3 cups flour
1 teaspoon baking soda
¼ teaspoon salt
3 tablespoons sugar
1¼ cups buttermilk or soured milk*
½ cup currants (optional)

Preheat oven to 375° F. Grease a baking sheet.

In a mixing bowl, combine flour, baking soda, salt, and sugar. Stir in currants, if desired. Add buttermilk to form a sticky dough. Place dough on a floured surface. Flour your hands, and knead the dough until it is smooth.

Place the dough on a baking sheet and form into a round, about 2 inches high. Using a knife, make a large X in the top of the dough. Bake for about 40 minutes.

Slice and serve with butter, jam, or lemon curd.

*To make soured milk: Place 1 tablespoon lemon juice in a measuring cup and add milk to make 1¼ cup of liquid. Mix, then allow to sit for about 5 minutes.

Coffee Cake

Great for a weekend brunch.

TOPPING:
½ cup flour
½ cup brown sugar,
   firmly packed
1 teaspoon ground cinnamon
¼ cup butter or margarine

BATTER:
2 cups flour
¾ cup sugar
3 teaspoons baking powder
1 teaspoon salt
1 egg
¼ cup vegetable oil
1 cup milk
1 teaspoon vanilla extract

Preheat the oven to 375° F. (350° F. if you are using a glass pan). Grease an 8-inch baking pan and set aside.

In a medium-sized mixing bowl, prepare the topping by combining ½ cup flour, the brown sugar and cinnamon. Cut in the margarine with a pastry cutter (or two knives) until the mixture becomes crumbly. Set aside.

Prepare the batter by sifting together 2 cups flour, the sugar, baking powder and salt into a large mixing bowl. Make a well in the center of the dry ingredients.

In a separate smaller bowl, beat the egg slightly. Mix milk, vanilla extract, and vegetable oil with the egg. Pour this mixture all at once into the center of the dry ingredients. Stir the batter just until the dry ingredients are moistened (about 20 strokes), scraping the bowl as you do so. Avoid over-mixing the batter.

Pour the batter into the prepared pan and sprinkle with the topping. Bake about 40 minutes, or until a toothpick inserted in the center of the cake comes out clean. Allow the coffeecake to cool in the pan.

Makes about 9 servings.

Peanut Butter Cake

Moist, delicious, and wonderfully fun!

1 cup flour
½ cup brown sugar, firmly packed
¼ cup granulated sugar
1 teaspoon baking powder
⅛ teaspoon baking soda
½ teaspoon salt
3 tablespoons butter or margarine,
  softened
¼ cup peanut butter,
  creamy or chunk style
½ cup milk
1 egg
½ teaspoon vanilla

Preheat the oven to 350° F. (325° F. if you are using a glass pan). Grease an 8-inch round or square baking pan and set aside.

Sift the flour, sugars, baking powder, baking soda and salt together into a mixing bowl. Add butter, peanut butter, and ¼ cup of the milk. Stir until blended, then beat until batter is smooth. Add eggs, vanilla, and the remaining ¼ cup milk. Beat until smooth and creamy.

Pour into the prepared pan. Bake until cake tests done (about 35 minutes).

If you wish, you may frost the cake with your favorite frosting once the it has cooled completely. Or, sift a little powdered sugar over the top while cake is still warm.

This recipe can be doubled and cake baked in a 9x13-inch baking pan, or baked in two 8-inch round cake pans to make a layer cake.

Scones

4 cups flour
½ cup sugar
2 tablespoons baking powder
2 teaspoons salt
½ cup vegetable oil
1⅓ cups milk
2 eggs
½ cup currants (optional)

Preheat oven to 375° F.

In a large mixing bowl, stir together the flour, sugar, baking powder and salt with a spoon or wire whisk. If you want currants in your scones, add the currants now. Make a well in the center of the dry ingredients.

In a separate smaller bowl, mix together the milk, eggs, and cooking oil. Pour this into the center of the dry ingredients and stir together until all the ingredients are moistened and the mixture has formed a soft dough.

Place the dough onto a lightly floured board. Dust your hands and the dough lightly with flour to keep the dough from sticking to your hands. Knead the dough gently, 20 times.

With a floured rolling pin, roll the dough into a 10-inch circle; or, with flour on your hands, you may pat the dough evenly into a 10-inch circle.

Cut the dough into 8 wedges, and place the wedges onto an ungreased baking sheet, leaving an inch or two between each wedge. Bake for 30-35 minutes.

Makes 8 hearty breakfast-sized scones. Delicious with butter, jam, or lemon curd. Serve with hot tea.

If you wish, you may make smaller scones from this recipe. Divide the dough in half and pat or roll into two 8-inch circles. Cut each circle into 6 wedges. Bake at 425° for about 15 minutes.

Makes 12 tea-sized scones.

How To Make An Ideal Cup of Tea

For some people—notably the British—there are few things worse than an improperly made cup of tea; and few things better than a properly made cup of tea.

There are a wide variety of teas from many different lands, each with its own unique blend of tea leaves and spices designed to make the drinking of it a delightful experience.

Regardless of which tea you select, *how* you make the tea can drastically affect its flavor.

• Rinse the teapot or teacup with boiling water just before using.
• Use 1 teabag or 1 teaspoon of tea per serving.
• Be sure the water is boiling when it hits the teabag!
• Brew the tea about 3 to 5 minutes, but no longer.
• Serve with cream, sugar, and lemon.

Carrot Cake

A delightful way to eat your veggies!

1¼ cups flour
1 teaspoon baking powder
1 teaspoon ground cinnamon
½ teaspoon baking soda
½ teaspoon salt
½ cup butter or margarine, softened
¾ cup sugar
1 egg
1 cup peeled, grated carrot
   (about 2 large carrots)
½ teaspoon vanilla extract
½ cup milk
¼ cup chopped nuts (optional)

Preheat oven to 350° F. (325° F. if you are using a glass pan). Grease a 8-inch square baking pan.

In a small mixing bowl, combine flour, baking powder, cinnamon, baking soda, and salt. Set aside.

In a large mixing bowl, cream the butter and sugar until it is light and fluffy. Blend in the egg, grated carrots and vanilla extract. Beat in half of the dry ingredients, then add half of the milk. Beat in the remaining dry ingredients and then the rest of the milk. Add chopped nuts (if desired) and stir them into the mixture.

Pour the batter into the prepared pan. Bake 45 to 50 minutes, or until a wooden toothpick inserted in center of the cake comes out clean.

Allow the cake to cool in the pan.

Frost with Cream Cheese Frosting. Garnish with additional chopped nuts, if desired.

Cornbread

1 cup yellow corn meal
1 cup flour
2 tablespoons to ¼ cup sugar
  (depending on how sweet you
  like your cornbread)
1 tablespoon baking powder
1 teaspoon salt
⅓ cup vegetable oil
1 egg
1 cup milk

Preheat the oven to 400° F. (375° F. if you are using a glass pan). Grease an 8-inch square or round baking pan; or if you wish to make corn muffins, grease a muffin pan.

In a large mixing bowl, sift together the cornmeal, flour, sugar, salt, and baking powder, using a sifter or wire whisk. Make a well in the center of the dry ingredients.

In a separate smaller bowl, combine the egg, milk, and vegetable oil and mix well. Pour the wet ingredients into the center of the dry ingredients. Stir all together just until the dry ingredients are moistened, about 15 to 20 strokes; be careful not to over-mix. Pour the batter into the prepared baking pan (or muffin cups).

Bake 20 to 25 minutes, or until a toothpick inserted in center of the cornbread comes out clean.

Makes 9 servings. Delicious served warm with butter, honey, apple butter, or your favorite jam.

Pumpkin Bread

A fall favorite for breakfast or snacks

3 cups flour
2 teaspoons baking soda
2 teaspoons baking powder
1 teaspoon salt
1 teaspoon ground cinnamon
1 teaspoon ground nutmeg
1 cup chopped nuts (optional)
4 eggs
1¼ cups packed brown sugar
1 cup vegetable oil
1 16-oz. can (2 cups) of pumpkin

Preheat oven to 350° F. (325° if you are using glass pans).
Grease and flour two 9x5-inch loaf pans and set aside.

In a large mixing bowl, place the flour, baking powder, soda, salt, cinnamon, and nutmeg (and nuts, if desired). Stir together with a spoon or wire whisk. Make a well in the center of the dry ingredients and set aside.

In a separate bowl, beat together the eggs, sugar, vegetable oil and pumpkin until well blended. Pour this mixture into the first bowl and mix just until the dry ingredients are moistened. Be careful not to over-mix.

 Divide the batter between the two prepared loaf pans. Bake one hour or until a toothpick inserted in the center of a loaf comes out clean. Remove from pans; slice and serve.

Makes two loaves. Pumpkin bread is excellent served with cream cheese, warm or cold.

This recipe freezes well, so it can be made in advance and frozen until ready to use.

Blueberry   Muffins

2½ cups flour
2½ teaspoons baking powder
1 cup sugar
¼ teaspoon salt
1 cup buttermilk or soured milk
2 eggs, beaten
½ cup butter or margarine, melted
¼ teaspoon vanilla
1½ cup blueberries

Preheat oven to 400° F. Grease about 15 to 18 muffin cups.

In a large mixing bowl, sift together flour, baking powder, sugar and salt. Make a well in the center of the dry ingredients.

In a separate small mixing bowl, combine the buttermilk, eggs, melted butter, and vanilla extract. Mix well, and pour into the center of the dry ingredients. Mix all ingredients together, using about 20 strokes; the batter will be lumpy. Gently stir in the blueberries. Fill greased muffin cups and bake for 20 minutes, or until muffins test done.

Makes 15-18 muffins. Delicious served warm!

Pound Cake

½ cup butter or margarine, softened
1 cup sugar
¼ teaspoon salt
¾ teaspoons vanilla extract
2 eggs
1 cup + 6 tablespoons flour
¼ teaspoon baking powder
¼ teaspoon baking soda
½ cup buttermilk or soured milk*

Grease and flour a 9x5-inch loaf pan. Preheat oven to 325° F. (or 300° F. if you are using a glass pan).

In a large mixing bowl, cream together the butter, sugar, salt and vanilla until the mixture is fluffy. Add the eggs one at a time and beat until well blended.

In a separate smaller bowl, sift together the flour, baking powder and soda. Stir this flour mixture into the butter mixture a little at a time, alternately adding buttermilk.

Turn the batter into the prepared loaf pan. Bake 50 to 60 minutes or until a toothpick inserted in the center of the cake comes out clean.

Place the cake (still in the pan) on a wire rack and allow to cool for 10 minutes; then turn the cake out onto the wire rack and allow the cake to cool completely, top side up.

* To make soured milk, pour 1½ teaspoons lemon juice or vinegar into the measuring cup, then add milk to make ½ cup of liquid. Allow to sit for about 5 minutes.

Nutmeg Cake

1 cup flour
1 teaspoon ground nutmeg
½ teaspoon baking soda
½ teaspoon baking powder
⅛ teaspoon salt
2 tablespoons butter or margarine, softened
2 tablespoons shortening, softened
¾ cup sugar
¼ teaspoon vanilla extract
1 egg, beaten
½ cup buttermilk or soured milk*
Powdered sugar for topping (optional)

Preheat oven to 350° F. (325° F. if you are using a glass pan). Grease a 8x8-inch baking pan.

In a medium-sized mixing bowl, sift together the flour, nutmeg, baking soda, baking powder, and salt. Set aside. In a larger mixing bowl, cream together the butter or margarine and shortening. Gradually add sugar to the butter mixture, beating in until the mixture is light and fluffy. Mix in the eggs and vanilla extract.

Add the dry ingredients to the creamed mixture a little at a time, alternately adding buttermilk. Beat well after each addition.

Pour into prepared pan. Bake 35 to 40 minutes or until a toothpick inserted in the center of the cake comes out clean.

If you wish, sift powdered sugar over top.

* To make soured milk, pour 1½ teaspoons lemon juice or vinegar into the measuring cup, then add milk to make ½ cup of liquid. Allow to sit for about 5 minutes.

Angel Food Loaf Cake

A Heavenly dessert!

¾ cup egg whites, at room temperature
   (about 6 large egg whites)
1 teaspoon cream of tartar
½ teaspoon vanilla extract
⅛ teaspoon salt
⅓ cup sugar
⅓ cup flour

Preheat oven to 350° F. (325° F. if you are using a glass pan). Line the bottom of a loaf pan with waxed paper. Do *not* grease the loaf pan!

Place the egg whites, cream of tartar, vanilla extract, and salt in a large mixing bowl, preferably one that is metal or glass. With mixer at high speed, beat all together until the egg whites are foamy. Gradually sprinkle in sugar a little at a time, beating continually until the sugar is dissolved and the egg whites are beaten into a meringue that forms soft peaks when the beaters are lifted. (Do not add all the sugar at once, as this will collapse the meringue!)

Sift the flour over the beaten egg whites. Using a rubber spatula, fold the flour into the egg whites until the flour and egg whites are blended. Be very gentle as you do this, using a slow vertical motion.

Spoon the mixture into prepared loaf pan. Bake 30 minutes or until the top of the cake springs back when touched lightly.

Invert the pan and set it upside down above the counter, resting the edges of the pan on two other pans or heat-resistant objects. (The cake will not fall out.) Allow the cake to rest, upside down, and cool completely.

Using a metal spatula, loosen the cake from the sides of the loaf pan and empty the cake right-side-up onto a serving dish. Discard the waxed paper.

Cherry Nut Bread

2 cups flour
½ teaspoon salt
½ cup sugar
½ cup chopped nuts
3 teaspoons baking powder

1 cup milk
1 egg, beaten
3 tablespoons vegetable oil
⅓ cup chopped maraschino cherries, drained.

Preheat oven to 350° F. (325° F. if you are using a glass pan). Grease a 9x5-inch loaf pan.

In a large mixing bowl, sift together the flour, baking powder, salt, and sugar. Stir in the nuts. Make a well in the center of the dry ingredients.

In a separate bowl, combine the milk, vegetable oil, egg, and cherries. Pour this into the dry ingredients. Stir about 15-20 strokes until the dry ingredients are just moistened, scraping the sides of the bowl as you mix.

Turn out the batter into the prepared pan. Bake about 60 minutes, or until a toothpick inserted in the center of the loaf comes out clean. Let cool in pan for about 10 minutes, then remove from pan. Allow the loaf to cool completely on a wire rack before slicing.

17

Chocolate Chip Muffins

3 cups flour
6 tablespoons granulated sugar
6 tablespoons brown sugar,
   firmly packed
3 teaspoons baking powder
¾ teaspoon baking soda
¾ teaspoon salt
1 cup chocolate chips
   (mini chips work great!)
1 cup buttermilk or soured milk*
½ cup vegetable oil
1 egg

Preheat oven to 375° F. Grease 12 regular-sized muffin cups.

In a large mixing bowl, combine the flour, granulated sugar, brown sugar, baking powder, baking soda and salt. Stir in chocolate chips. Make a well in the center of these ingredients and set aside.

In a smaller mixing bowl, combine the milk, vegetable oil and egg. Pour this into dry ingredients. Stir all ingredients together until the dry ingredients are just moistened (the batter will be lumpy). Spoon the batter into prepared muffin cups.

Bake 18 to 21 minutes, or until muffins are golden and a toothpick inserted in the center of a muffin comes out clean.

Allow muffins to cool in the pan for 5 minutes, then remove from the pan. Makes 12 very tasty muffins!

* To make soured milk, pour 1 tablespoon lemon juice or vinegar into the measuring cup, then add fresh milk to make 1 cup of liquid. Allow to sit for about 5 minutes.

Banana Bread

1⅓ cups flour
1 teaspoon soda
¾ teaspoon salt
¾ teaspoon baking powder
½ cup sugar
6 tablespoons butter or margarine, softened
2 eggs, beaten
2 medium bananas, mashed (about 1¾ cups)

Preheat the oven to 325° F. (350° F. if you are using a glass pan.) Grease and flour a 9x5-inch loaf pan and set aside.

In a mixing bowl, combine together flour, salt, soda and baking powder.

In a larger mixing bowl, place butter or margarine and sugar. Cream together until light and fluffy. Mix in the eggs and bananas. Add the flour mixture to the banana mixture and mix well.

Turn batter into prepared loaf pan. Bake about 1 hour, or until a toothpick inserted in the center of the loaf comes out clean. If you can wait that long, allow banana bread to cool completely before slicing.

Banana Bread lends itself to many variations!

• For a nuttier treat, add:
   ½ cup chopped nuts

• For a light and tasty fruitcake, add:
   1 cup chopped candied fruit
   ½ to 1 cup chopped nuts

• Or, for a truly festive holiday bread, add:
   1 can mandarin orange sections,
      chopped and drained
   ½ cup semi-sweet chocolate chips
   ½ cup chopped almonds or other nuts
   ¼ cup maraschino cherries,
      chopped and drained

Marsha's Nut Dessert

A sweet, densely packed treat

1⅓ cups light brown sugar
1½ cups sifted flour
6 tablespoons soft butter or margarine
¼ teaspoon salt
¼ cup chopped pecans or other nuts
1 egg
¼ teaspoon vanilla extract
¾ cup sour cream
¾ teaspoon baking soda
1¾ cups coarsely chopped pecans
   or other nuts

Heat oven to 350° F. (325° F. if using a glass pan). Grease and lightly flour a 8-inch baking pan.

In a large mixing bowl, combine brown sugar, flour, and salt. Cut in the butter or margarine with a pastry blender until the mixture is well mixed and crumbly. Mix using your hands if needed to thoroughly combine ingredients.

Put 1½ cups of this mixture into a separate mixing bowl and stir in ¼ cups of chopped pecans (or other nuts). Press this mixture firmly and evenly into the bottom of the prepared pan. This will be the crust.

In a small bowl, mix the sour cream and baking soda. Stir this sour cream mixture into the remaining crumb mixture (in the first bowl). Mix in the egg and vanilla extract. Blend well, then pour onto the crust in the pan. Sprinkle the top with the remaining chopped pecans (or other nuts).

Bake for 1 hour or until a toothpick inserted into the center of the cake comes out clean.

Chocolate Delights

Decadent Chocolate Dessert

A chocolate indulgence that's very easy to make!

1¼ cups sugar
1 cup all-purpose flour
7 tablespoons unsweetened cocoa, sifted
2 teaspoons baking powder
¼ teaspoon salt
½ cup milk
⅓ cup butter or margarine, melted
1½ teaspoons vanilla extract
½ cup packed light brown sugar
1¼ cups hot water

Preheat the oven to 350° F. (325° F. if using a glass pan).

In a medium-sized mixing bowl, combine ¾ cup of the sugar, the flour, 3 tablespoons of cocoa, baking powder and salt. Mix in the milk, melted butter and vanilla, and beat until smooth. Pour the batter into an 8-inch square baking pan or a 2-quart casserole dish.

In a small bowl, combine the remaining ½ cup sugar, the brown sugar and the remaining 4 tablespoons of cocoa. Sprinkle this mixture evenly over the batter. Pour hot water over the top, but do *not* stir the water into the batter!

Bake 40 minutes, until the top is firm and brownie-like. Remove from oven and allow to cool for 15 minutes before serving.

Makes 8 to 10 servings. This dessert is delicious warm or cold, and is exceptionally good when served with whipped topping or vanilla ice cream!

Chocolate Cheesecake

1½ lbs. cream cheese, softened
  (three 8-oz. packages)
1¼ cups sugar
¼ cup unsweetened cocoa, sifted
½ cup sour cream
2 teaspoons vanilla extract
2 tablespoons flour
3 eggs

Heat oven to 450° F. Grease an 8-inch springform pan or a 2-qt baking dish.

In a large mixing bowl, combine the cream cheese, sugar, cocoa, sour cream and vanilla; beat with an electric mixer until smooth. Add the flour and eggs, and beat well. Pour this mixture into the prepared pan, and bake for 10 minutes.

Without opening the oven, reduce temperature to 250° F., and continue baking for 30 minutes. At this point the cheesecake will be done, although it may not appear set (firm) in the center. Turn off the oven, and let the cheesecake set for another 30 minutes with the door closed.

Remove the cheesecake from the oven. If you are using a springform pan, loosen the cheesecake from the side of the pan with a knife. Cool the cheesecake to room temperature, then remove the sides of the springform pan.

Refrigerate the cheesecake for at least three hours. If you wish, you may garnish the cheesecake with chocolate curls or sliced fruit and whipped cream. Cover and refrigerate any leftover cheesecake.

Makes 10 to 12 servings.

Variations: If you wish, you can make this cheesecake in combination with your favorite graham cracker crust recipe. The recipe can also be halved and baked in an 8-inch round cake pan, with or without crust. (Use 2 eggs if halving recipe.)

Mississippi Mud

A traditional favorite from the south

2 eggs
½ cup butter or margarine, softened
1 cup sugar
½ teaspoon vanilla extract
¾ cup flour
2 tablespoons unsweetened cocoa, sifted
A dash of salt
½ cup chopped pecans or other nuts
¾ cup marshmallow creme

FROSTING:
3 tablespoons butter or margarine
¼ cup unsweetened cocoa, sifted
3 tablespoons milk
½ teaspoon vanilla extract
1¼ cups powdered sugar, sifted

Preheat oven to 350° F. (or 325° F. if using a glass pan). Grease a 8-inch square baking pan; set aside.

In a small mixing bowl, combine the flour, cocoa, and salt. In a large mixing bowl beat together the eggs, butter, sugar and vanilla until the mixture is light and fluffy. Add the cocoa mixture and beat until it is just moistened, then fold in the pecans.

Spread the batter evenly in the prepared pan. Bake for 35 to 40 minutes.

Remove the cake from oven and *immediately* place dollops of marshmallow creme over the hot cake. Spread out the marshmallow creme until it is smooth. Set the cake (in the pan) on a wire rack and allow to cool completely — at least one hour.

In a medium saucepan over medium heat, melt the butter or margarine. Sift in the cocoa and cook and stir 1 minute. Remove the pan from the heat, and stir in the milk and vanilla extract. Sift in the powdered sugar and stir briskly until the mixture is smooth.

When the cake has cooled, spread the frosting over the top of the marshmallow creme. Cut the cake into squares. (This dessert is very rich, so cut it into *small* squares.)

Makes 8-24 servings, depending on your greed.

Mocha Drops

2½ cups flour
½ teaspoon baking powder
½ teaspoon salt
1 tablespoon powdered instant coffee
6 tablespoons unsweetened cocoa, sifted
7 tablespoons shortening
6 oz. cream cheese, softened
1 cup sugar
1 egg
1½ teaspoons vanilla extract

Preheat oven to 375° F. In a small mixing bowl, combine flour, baking powder, salt, instant coffee, and cocoa. In a large mixing bowl, blend shortening and cream cheese together thoroughly. Add sugar and blend well. Add egg and vanilla extract. Gradually add dry ingredients to creamed mixture.

Drop by heaping teaspoonfuls onto ungreased cookie sheet and bake for 10 to 12 minutes. Remove to wire racks to cool.

Steamed Chocolate Pudding

Moist and rich!

1 cup sugar

10 tablespoons butter or margarine, softened

2 eggs

1 teaspoon vanilla extract

1½ cup flour

6 tablespoons unsweetened cocoa, sifted

1¼ teaspoon baking powder

¼ teaspoon baking soda

¼ teaspoon salt

½ cup milk

¾ cup chopped nuts

Extra cocoa for use in dusting the pudding mold

Grease a 4-cup pudding mold or stainless steel mixing bowl. Dust the inside of the greased bowl or pudding mold with cocoa. Set aside.

In a large mixing bowl, cream the sugar and butter until the mixture is light and fluffy. Add the eggs and vanilla extract, and beat until the mixture is smooth.

In a separate bowl, mix the flour, sifted cocoa, baking powder, baking soda and salt. Once thoroughly combined, beat half of this flour mixture into the creamed mixture, then beat in half of the milk. Beat in the remaining flour mixture, then the rest of the milk. Stir in chopped nuts.

Prepare a steamer: Place a trivet inside a large pot — large enough to easily contain the cocoa-dusted bowl or pudding mold. An inverted disposable aluminum pie pan, with holes punched in it, will work as a trivet.

Pour the batter into the mold. Place a double thickness of foil over the mold and secure it with a length of string. Place the mold on the trivet inside the large pot, and pour boiling water into the pot until the level of the water is halfway up the sides of the pudding mold. Cover the pot and simmer for 1 hour.

Remove the mold from the pot and set it on a wire rack. Let the pudding cool completely, then invert the mold to plop the pudding onto a platter. (If the pudding sticks in the mold, loosen by briefly dipping the mold in hot water.)

Makes 6-8 generous servings.

Choco-Nut Pie

½ cup butter or margarine, softened
⅔ cup brown sugar, firmly packed
3 eggs
¼ cup granulated sugar
1 teaspoon vanilla extract
¼ cup molasses
1 tablespoon flour
⅓ cup chopped pecans or other nuts
½ cup chocolate chips
1 9-inch unbaked pie crust
   or graham cracker crust

Heat oven to 350° F.

In a mixing bowl, beat together the butter and sugar until the combination is light and fluffy. Add the eggs one at a time, beating well after each addition. Add salt, vanilla, and molasses, and blend well.

In a separate bowl, sprinkle the flour over the pecans and gently toss the mixture to dust the pecans with the flour. Mix the pecans, flour and chocolate chips into the filling mixture, and blend well.

Pour the filling into a prepared pie shell. If you are using a pastry crust rather than a graham cracker crust, you may wish to take a thin strip of aluminum foil and cover the edges of the pie shell to prevent the crust from overbrowning. (Do *not* cover the filling.)

Bake 35-40 minutes, or until a knife inserted into the center of the pie comes out clean. Allow pie to cool completely before serving.

Makes 8 wonderfully rich servings.

Cocoa Balls

1 cup flour
¼ cup unsweetened cocoa, sifted
A dash of salt
½ cup butter or margarine, softened
⅓ cup sugar
⅛ teaspoon vanilla extract
½ cup chopped nuts
4½ teaspoons unsweetened cocoa, sifted
4½ teaspoons powdered sugar, sifted

In a medium mixing bowl combine flour, ¼ cup cocoa and salt. Set aside. In a large mixing bowl, cream butter and sugar together; beat until light and fluffy. Gradually add dry ingredients and vanilla extract and beat just until well blended. Stir in nuts. Cover dough and chill at least 1 hour.

Preheat oven to 350° F. Shape cookie dough into 1-inch balls. Place on ungreased cookie sheets. Bake 12 minutes. Let stand on cookie sheets 2 to 3 minutes before removing to wire racks to cool.

In a small bowl, sift together powdered sugar and remaining cocoa. When cookies have cooled enough to handle, roll cookies in cocoa mixture.

Chocolate Mousse

1 envelope unflavored gelatin
2½ cups milk
¼ cup unsweetened cocoa, sifted
1 tablespoon cornstarch
1 egg
1 teaspoon vanilla extract
¼ cup sugar
1 cup whipped topping or whipped cream

Put the milk in a medium saucepan. Sprinkle gelatin over the milk and it let stand 5 minutes to soften the gelatin. Stir in the egg, sugar, cocoa, and cornstarch. Cook over medium heat, stirring constantly with a wire whisk, until the mixture comes to a boil. Reduce heat to low and continue stirring until the mixture thickens. This should take only a few minutes.

Remove from heat and allow the mixture to cool until it is lukewarm. Stir in vanilla. Pour the mixture into a serving bowl and refrigerate. Stir the mixture occasionally until it is thickened (about 45 minutes).

Gently fold 1 cup of prepared whipped topping into the chocolate mixture. Cover and refrigerate until firm.

French Silk Pie

1 cup butter or margarine, softened
¾ cup sugar
1½ teaspoons vanilla extract
¼ teaspoon cream of tartar
9 tablespoons unsweetened cocoa, sifted
1 cup pasteurized egg (such as *Egg Beaters*)*****
1 9-inch baked pie shell, or 1 prepared graham cracker crust
1 cup whipped cream or whipped topping (optional)

Place the butter in a large mixing bowl and beat in the sugar a little at a time. Mix in the vanilla, cream of tartar and cocoa. Add the pasteurized 'egg' ¼ cup at a time, beating 3 minutes after each addition; scrape the sides of the bowl often.

Pour the mixture into the prepared pie shell. Cover with plastic wrap and refrigerate 3 to 4 hours or until set. (The pie can be safely frozen, allow 15 minutes to thaw a frozen pie.) Remove the plastic wrap when ready to serve.

As an option, add whipped topping or sprinkle the top with grated chocolate or semi-sweet chocolate chips.

* - because no cooking is involved, an egg substitute is recommended instead of raw eggs, to prevent the possibility of Salmonella poisoning.

Brownies

½ cup butter or margarine, melted
¾ cup sugar
1 teaspoon vanilla
2 eggs
6 tablespoons unsweetened cocoa, sifted
½ cup flour
¼ teaspoon baking powder
⅛ teaspoon salt
½ chopped nuts (optional)

Heat oven to 350° F. (or to 325° F. for a glass baking pan). Grease an 8-inch square baking pan and set aside.

In a mixing bowl, combine melted butter, sugar and vanilla. Add the eggs one at a time, beating well with spoon after each addition. Add the cocoa and beat until it is well blended. Add flour, baking powder and salt; beat well. Stir in nuts, if desired.

Pour batter into prepared pan. Bake 30 to 35 minutes or until brownies begin to pull away from sides of pan.

Let the brownies cool completely in the pan atop a wire rack. Cut into bars to serve.

Double Chocolate Cookies

The chocoholic's chocolate chip cookie!

1¾ cup flour
½ cup unsweetened cocoa, sifted
¾ teaspoon baking soda
½ teaspoon baking powder
¼ teaspoon salt
¾ cup butter or margarine, softened
¾ cup sugar
½ cup light brown sugar, packed
1 teaspoon vanilla extract
2 eggs
1 cup chocolate chips
½ cup chopped nuts

Preheat oven to 375° F.

In a small mixing bowl, stir together the flour, cocoa, baking soda, baking powder and salt. Set aside.

In a large mixing bowl, mix the butter, sugar, brown sugar and vanilla extract. Beat the mixture until it is well blended. Add the eggs, and beat well.

Gradually add the flour mixture to the butter mixture, beating just until blended; do not over-mix. Add the chocolate chips and nuts, and stir gently.

Drop the dough by heaping teaspoonfuls onto an ungreased cookie sheet. Bake 7 minutes, or until the cookies are done. Cool 1 minute on the cookie sheet, then remove the cookies from the cookie sheet to a wire rack to cool completely.

Black Forest Brownies

A famous variation on your basic brownie

BROWNIE LAYER:
¾ cup flour
6 tablespoons rolled oats
½ teaspoon baking powder
⅛ teaspoon salt
¼ cup unsweetened cocoa, sifted
6 tablespoons margarine, melted
⅔ cup sugar
½ teaspoon vanilla extract
1 egg
½ cup chopped maraschino cherries

TOPPING:
¼ cup chocolate chips
1 teaspoon shortening
8 whole Maraschino cherries

Heat oven to 350° F. (325° F. if you are using a glass pan). Lightly grease an 8- inch square baking pan and set aside.

In a mixing bowl, combine the flour, oatmeal, baking powder, salt, and cocoa.

In a small pan, melt the butter, then pour this into a separate mixing bowl and add the sugar and vanilla extract. Add the egg and beat well.

Add the dry ingredients to the wet mixture and mix thoroughly, then stir in the chopped cherries. Spread the combined mix into the greased pan. Bake about 25 minutes, or until the brownies pull away from the sides of the pan. Remove from the oven and allow to cool completely in the pan.

Cut the brownies into 16 squares. Cut the 8 whole Maraschino cherries in half and place one half-cherry on the center of each brownie. In a saucepan over low heat (or in the microwave), slowly melt the chocolate chips and vegetable shortening and stir until smooth. Drizzle this melted mixture over the cooled brownies and cherry halves, and allow to cool.

Store tightly covered.

Variations: when adding the chopped cherries, also add ¼ cup chopped nuts and/or ¼ cup semi-sweet chocolate chips.

Alpine Brownies

Follow the directions for *Black Forest Brownies*; [b]ut before adding the half-cherries and chocolate [d]rizzle, frost the brownies with this recipe:

tablespoons shortening, softened

[¼] teaspoon salt

teaspoon vanilla extract (or other flavoring)

tablespoons milk

½ cups powdered sugar, sifted

In a small mixing bowl, mix the shortening, salt, [fl]avoring, and ¾ cup of the powdered sugar, beating [al]l together with a spoon or electric mixer. Add milk, [al]ternately adding the rest of the powdered sugar. Mix [u]ntil smooth and creamy. Add more powdered sugar [if] the frosting is too thin; if the frosting is too thick to [s]pread, add a little more milk.

After frosting the brownies, top with the half-[c]herries and drizzle with chocolate glaze, as before.

Chocolate Fudge

⅔ cup unsweetened cocoa, sifted
3 cups sugar
⅛ teaspoon salt
1½ cups milk
¼ cup butter
1 teaspoon vanilla

Lightly butter an 8-inch pan and set aside.

In a 4-quart saucepan, combine the sifted cocoa, sugar, and salt. Gradually add milk and mix well.

Slowly bring the mixture to a bubbly boil over medium heat, stirring constantly. When the mixture starts boiling, clip a candy thermometer to the side of the pan, taking care that the bulb of the thermometer does not touch the bottom of the pan. Continue to boil, without stirring, until the temperature reaches 234° F. (also known as the 'soft ball stage*'). Leave in the candy thermometer and remove the saucepan from heat. Place butter and vanilla on top of mixture, but do *not* stir!

Cool the mixture to 110° F. (You should be able to easily touch the bottom of the pan.) Beat the butter and vanilla into the fudge by hand, and keep beating until the fudge thickens and looks less glossy. Just as it starts to thicken, quickly spread the fudge into the prepared pan.

Allow the fudge to cool completely, then cut it into 1-inch squares.

*If you do not have a candy thermometer, test the fudge mixture by dropping a small amount into a cup of ice-cold water. If the mixture forms a soft ball in the water, the fudge has reached "soft-ball" stage and is ready for the next step in the recipe.

Chocolate Mint Bars

BROWNIE LAYER:

1 cup sugar

⅔ cup butter or margarine, softened

2 eggs

1 teaspoon vanilla

¾ cups flour

¾ teaspoons salt

½ teaspoon baking powder

7 tablespoons unsweetened cocoa, sifted

1 cup coarsely chopped nuts

MINT FROSTING

2 cups powdered sugar, sifted

2 tablespoons butter or margarine, softened

1 tablespoon milk

½ teaspoon mint extract

Green food coloring (optional)

CHOCOLATE GLAZE

3 tablespoons unsweetened cocoa, sifted

2 tablespoons shortening

Preheat oven to 350° F. (325° if you are using a glass pan). Grease an 8-inch square baking pan and set aside.

In a large mixing bowl, cream together the softened butter and sugar. Beat in the eggs and vanilla extract. In a separate bowl, stir together the flour, sugar, salt, and baking powder. Sift in the cocoa and mix thoroughly.

Add the dry ingredients to the sugar mixture and mix well. Fold in nuts. Spread the batter in the prepared pan. Bake for 35 to 40 minutes until a toothpick inserted in the center comes out with fudgy crumbs; be careful not to overbake! Allow to cool completely.

In a separate mixing bowl, thoroughly combine all frosting ingredients. If needed, add a little more milk, ½ a teaspoon at a time, until the frosting is a good consistency for spreading. Spread the frosting over the cooled brownie layer.

Place the frosted brownies in the freezer for 15 to 20 minutes to allow the frosting to harden. Cut the brownies into bars, but do not remove from pan.

Prepare the glaze by melting the shortening and butter in a small saucepan or in the microwave. Sift in the cocoa and blend thoroughly. Brush the glaze evenly on top of mint frosting. Refrigerate to harden glaze, then carefully re-cut the bars.

Store in tightly covered container, layered with sheets of waxed paper.

Chocolate Truffles

¾ cup butter or margarine
¾ cup unsweetened cocoa, sifted
1 can (14 oz.) sweetened condensed milk
1 tablespoon vanilla extract
Suggested Coatings:
    Unsweetened cocoa
    Powdered sugar
    Unsweetened cocoa mixed with powdered sugar
    Chopped nuts
    ½ cup semi-sweet chocolate chips,
        melted with 1 teaspoon shortening

Melt the butter in a heavy saucepan over low heat. Sift in the cocoa and stir until smooth. Blend in the sweetened condensed milk.

Stir the mixture until it just starts to bubble. Continue

stirring for about 4 or 5 minutes until the mixture is thick, smooth, and glossy — about the consistency of thick frosting. Remove from heat and stir in vanilla. Let cool, then refrigerate 3 to 4 hours or until firm.

With a teaspoon or melon baller, shape the chilled chocolate mixture into small balls about ¾ inch diameter; these are the truffle centers.

Using a spoon, roll the truffle centers in a small dish containing the coating (or coatings!) of your choice. If the truffle centers become too soft to roll smoothly, refrigerate them again for 20 minutes.

Refrigerate the finished, coated truffles for 1 to 2 hours or until firm. Keep refrigerated until ready to serve.

For chocolate-covered truffles, cover a baking sheet with waxed paper. Melt the chocolate chips and shortening together in a small pan or in the microwave. Roll the chilled truffle centers in the melted chocolate mixture, then set it on the waxed paper. Place the baking sheet in the refrigerator and allow the truffles to chill until firm.

Chocolate Puffs
Airy and delicious!

1 egg white at room temperature
A dash of salt
¼ teaspoon vinegar
¼ teaspoon vanilla extract
¼ cup granulated sugar
½ cup semi-sweet chocolate chips, melted and cooled
⅓ cup chopped walnuts or other nuts (optional)

Preheat oven to 350° F. and grease a cookie sheet.

Place the egg white, salt, vinegar, and vanilla in a mixing bowl (preferably a glass or metal mixing bowl.) Beat with an egg beater or electric mixer until the mixture forms soft peaks when the beater is lifted. Gradually add sugar, a little at a time, beating after each addition; do *not* add the sugar all at once! Beat until the mixture is glossy, and stiff peaks form when the beater is lifted.

Gently fold melted chocolate and nuts into the mixture. Drop from teaspoon onto the greased cookie sheet. Bake for about 10 minutes and allow to cool.

Chocolate Cake

1 cup flour
½ cup white sugar
6 tablespoons unsweetened cocoa, sifted
¾ teaspoon baking soda
¾ teaspoon baking powder
½ teaspoon salt
½ cup + 2 tablespoons buttermilk
  or soured milk*
½ cup packed light brown sugar
1 egg, lightly beaten
2 tablespoons vegetable oil
1 teaspoon pure vanilla extract
1 tablespoon instant coffee
  dissolved in ½ cup hot water

Preheat oven to 350° F. (325° F. if using a glass pan). Grease and flour an 8-inch square pan.

In a large mixing bowl, mix together the flour, white sugar, cocoa, baking soda, baking powder and salt. Add the buttermilk, brown sugar, egg, vegetable oil and vanilla, and beat vigorously for 2 minutes. Add the prepared hot coffee until the batter is completely mixed. (The batter will be quite thin.)

Pour the batter into the greased, floured pan. Bake for 35 to 40 minutes, or until a toothpick inserted in the center comes out clean.

Allow the cake to cool completely before serving.

You may frost this cake if you wish with your choice of frostings — but this cake is so moist and so chocolatey, it is delicious by itself!

* To make soured milk, pour 1½ teaspoons lemon juice or vinegar into the measuring cup, then add milk to make the required amount of liquid. Allow to sit for about 5 minutes.

Layers of Heaven

Cocoa, chocolate, cocoa and chocolate — how can you go wrong?!

BOTTOM LAYER:

½ cup chopped pecans or other nuts

1 cup flour

½ cup + 2 tablespoons butter or margarine, softened

¼ cup sugar

3 tablespoons unsweetened cocoa, sifted

MIDDLE LAYER:

1 cup cold milk

1 3-oz. package of instant chocolate pudding

TOP LAYER:

6 oz. cream cheese, softened

½ cup powdered sugar

¼ cup unsweetened cocoa, sifted

1 cup prepared whipped topping or whipped cream

GARNISH:

1 cup prepared whipped topping or whipped cream

¼ cup chopped pecans or other nuts

2 tablespoons chocolate chips or grated chocolate

Preheat oven to 350° F. (325° F. if you are using a glass pan).

Bottom layer: In a large mixing bowl, mix together the bottom layer ingredients, kneading them together with your hands if necessary until thoroughly combined. Pat the mixture into an 8x8-inch square pan and bake for 25 minutes. Allow to cool.

Middle layer: Prepare the instant pudding according to package directions, using only 1 cup of milk. Spread this over the cooled bottom layer.

Top layer: Place the cream cheese in a mixing bowl. Sift the powdered sugar and cocoa over the cream cheese and beat until thoroughly combined. Add the whipped topping to the bowl and mix together. Spread this over the middle layer.

Garnish: place dollops of whipped cream over the top layer and spread out evenly. Sprinkle with chopped nuts and your choice of grated chocolate or chocolate chips.

Makes 6-8 servings. Best served thoroughly chilled.

Peanut Butter Brownies

BOTTOM LAYER:

6 tablespoons unsweetened cocoa, sifted

½ cup butter or margarine, melted

1 cup sugar

1 egg

½ teaspoon vanilla extract

½ cup flour

½ cup chopped peanuts

TOP LAYER:

½ cup peanut butter

¼ cup powdered sugar, sifted

½ teaspoon vanilla extract

GLAZE:

6 tablespoons unsweetened cocoa, sifted

4 tablespoons shortening

Heat oven to 350° F. (325° F. if you are using a glass pan). Grease an 8-inch square baking pan and set aside.

Bottom Layer: In a mixing bowl, sift the cocoa into the melted butter. Stir in the sugar. Add the egg and 1 teaspoon vanilla, and beat until well blended. Add flour and peanuts, and stir until thoroughly mixed.

Spread the mixture into the prepared pan. Bake for 25 to 30 minutes, or until a toothpick inserted into center comes out with fudgy crumbs; be careful not to overbake! Allow the bottom layer to cool in the pan.

Top Layer: In a separate mixing bowl, mix the peanut butter, powdered sugar and vanilla until the mixture is blended and smooth. Spread over the cooled bottom layer.

Glaze: Melt the shortening in a small saucepan over low heat, or in the microwave. Sift in the cocoa and mix well. Spread or brush the glaze over the top layer. Refrigerate until the glaze is cool and firm.

Cut into squares and serve chilled.

Serves 8-16, depending on your level of greed.

Fruit Desserts

Nature's Brown Betty

A delicious dessert that's filled with healthy stuff!

4 tart baking apples
¼ cup raisins or dried currants (optional)
¼ cup honey
¼ cup apple juice or water
¼ cup brown sugar
4½ teaspoons white flour
½ teaspoon ground cinnamon
TOPPING:
¼ cup rolled oats
¼ cup whole wheat flour
¼cup wheat germ
¼ cup shelled sunflower seeds
2 tablespoons honey
2 tablespoons butter or margarine,
   softened

Preheat oven to 350° F. (325° F. if you are using a glass pan). Lightly grease an 8-inch square baking pan.

Peel and core the apples, and cut them into slices. Place the apple slices in a large mixing bowl. Add raisins, honey, apple juice, brown sugar, flour, and cinnamon, and mix well. Spread the batter into the prepared pan.

In a separate mixing bowl, combine the oats, flour, wheat germ, and sunflower seeds. Cut the butter into the mixture using a pastry cutter or two knives. Blend until the margarine is evenly distributed, then add the honey and again stir well.

Spread the oat mixture over the apple mixture. Bake 45-50 minutes or until the apples are tender.

Best served warm — and *really* best when topped with ice cream!

Country Cobbler

FRUIT FILLING:

1 tablespoon corn starch
3 cups fresh fruit, peeled and cut into
    bite-size pieces (include natural juice,
    if any)
½ to 1 cup sugar (depending on
    sweetness of fruit)
1 tablespoon butter or margarine
Ground cinnamon

TOPPING:

1 cup flour
1 tablespoon sugar
1 tablespoon baking powder
½ teaspoon salt
3 tablespoons shortening
¾ cup milk

Preheat oven to 400° F. (or 375° F. if you are using a glass pan). Grease a 1½-qt. baking dish.

In a mixing bowl, mix the sugar and cornstarch with the fruit and juice. Pour this into the prepared baking dish. Lay small slices of the butter or margarine on top of the fruit, then sprinkle it all with cinnamon.

In a separate bowl, mix together the topping ingredients: flour, sugar, baking powder, and salt. Cut in the shortening with a pastry blender or two knives until the mixture looks like coarse grain. Stir in milk. Using a spoon, drop this mixture onto the fruit.

Bake for 25-30 minutes, or until the topping is just golden brown. Serve warm. Makes 6 to 8 servings.

For an added treat, top this with ice cream or whipped topping.

Cornbread Berry Cobbler

COBBLER:
1 quart fresh strawberries or blackberries, washed
½ cup sugar

SAUCE:
¼ cup honey
1 tablespoon melted butter or margarine
1 tablespoon lemon juice

TOPPING:
1 cup corn meal
¼ cup sugar
1 teaspoon baking powder
1 teaspoon salt
½ cup sour milk or buttermilk
1 egg
2 tablespoons melted butter or margarine

Preheat oven to 375° F. (or 350° if you are using a glass pan).

If you are using strawberries, slice them in half. Place the berries in a 2-quart baking dish, and sprinkle with sugar.

For the topping: mix together all dry ingredients in a large mixing bowl, using a spoon or wire whisk. Quickly stir in the sour milk, egg, and melted butter or margarine. Use a tablespoon to drop the batter mixture onto the berries, creating a random pattern.

In a smaller bowl, mix together the sauce ingredients, and pour over batter and exposed berries.

Bake for 1 hour. Serve at room temperature.

Makes 6-8 servings.

This goes very well topped with cream, whipped topping or ice cream!

Cherry Pudding
Super-good and super-easy!

½ cup butter or margarine
1½ cups sugar
1 cup flour
2 teaspoons baking powder
¾ cup milk
1 1-lb. can pitted cherries

Preheat oven to 325° F. (or 300° F. if you are using a glass pan).

Place the butter in an 8-inch square baking pan. Set the pan in the oven and allow the butter to melt, then remove the pan from the oven.

In a mixing bowl, combine the 1 cup of sugar, the flour, baking powder, and milk. Mix until well blended. Pour the mixture over the melted butter, but do not stir. Pour undrained cherries and juice over the batter; again, do not stir. Sprinkle the remaining ½ cup sugar over the cherries, but still no stirring!! Bake for 1 hour.

Makes 8 servings, unstirred.

Almond Creme with Raspberry Sauce

A delicate dish with a tangy topping!

ALMOND CREME:

1 package unflavored gelatin
¼ cup cold water
¼ cup boiling water
2 cups evaporated milk or
　　whipping cream
⅓ cup honey
1 teaspoon almond extract

RASPBERRY SAUCE:

1 cup raspberries, fresh or frozen
¼ cup sugar
2 teaspoons cornstarch

In a mixing bowl, soften the gelatin in the cold water. Add boiling water; stir until dissolved. Add the cream, honey, and extract, and stir until mixed. Pour the creme mixture into 6 dessert dishes, and chill for 3 to 4 hours or until firm.

If the raspberries are frozen, thaw and drain them (but save the liquid). Place half of the raspberries in a saucepan. Put the drained liquid from the raspberries in a measuring cup, and add enough water to make ½ cup of liquid. Add the liquid, sugar, and cornstarch to the berries in the saucepan. Cook and stir until the mixture is bubbly; then cook 2 minutes more. Add the remaining raspberries and stir gently. Once mixed, remove the raspberry sauce from the heat. Cover and chill the raspberry sauce.

Spoon the raspberry sauce over the creme and serve as is, in the dish. Alternately, you may dip the creme dishes quickly in hot water to loosen the creme, turn out the molded creme onto a serving plates and spoon raspberry sauce over the creme.

Makes 6 delicious servings.

Pear Brown Betty

3 cups ¼-inch bread cubes
4 tablespoons butter or margarine,
  melted
2 16-oz. cans sliced pears
¾ cup brown sugar, packed
1 teaspoon vanilla extract

Heat oven to 350° F. (325° F. if you are using a glass dish). Lightly butter an 8-inch square baking pan and set aside.

In a large bowl, combine the bread cubes and the melted butter, gently tossing the bread cubes until they are coated. Drain the pears, reserving ½ cup of their juice. In a medium bowl, add ⅔ cup of the sugar, the pears and the vanilla, and mix until the sugar dissolves.

Scatter ⅓ of the bread cubes on the bottom of the pan. Arrange half the pear mixture on top. Add another layer of bread, the remaining pears, and a final layer of bread. Pour juice over all.

Cover tightly with foil. Bake 30 minutes. Remove cover, sprinkle remaining 2 tablespoons of sugar over top. Bake uncovered for 30 minutes or until top is lightly browned.

Makes 6-8 servings. Best served warm.

Baked Apples

3 apples
½ cup of cold water mixed with 1½ teaspoons cornstarch

FILLING:
½ teaspoon ground cinnamon
2 tablespoons butter or margarine, softened
3 tablespoons brown sugar
3 tablespoons chopped nuts (optional)
3 tablespoons raisins, currants, or chopped dates (optional)

Preheat oven to 375° F.

Cut the apples in half, lengthwise. Cut the core out of each half and place the apples in a baking dish, open-side up.

Combine the filling ingredients in a small bowl. Press a spoonful of the filling firmly into the cored center of each apple half. Sprinkle some extra brown sugar over the top of the apple halves. Pour the cornstarch and water mixture into the pan. Add more water as needed so that the apples are resting in about ¼ inch of water.

Bake the apples about 50 to 55 minutes, spooning the liquid in the baking dish over them occasionally. Serve hot with some of the syrup in the pan spooned over.

Ye Olde Apple Pudding

A Renaissance favorite

12 slices (more or less) of white bread
  with crusts removed
Butter or margarine
1 cup fresh white bread crumbs
3 tablespoons sifted powdered sugar
4 or 5 firm, sweet apples — peeled, cored
  and chopped
Finely grated zest and juice of 1 lemon
  (or 3 tablespoons lemon juice)
Pinch of ground cloves
3 tablespoons granulated sugar

Preheat oven to 375° F. (350° F. if you are using a glass dish). Lightly grease a 5-cup baking dish.

Or, if you prefer, line the baking dish with well-greased wax paper, to aid in unmolding the apple pudding.

Sift powdered sugar onto a large plate. Butter the bread slices, and dredge the buttered side of the bread through the powdered sugar.

Line the prepared baking dish with bread slices, sugared side facing inward. Overlap each piece slightly, without creating large overlaps; trim bread as necessary to make it fit. Reserve enough bread slices to make a lid. Set the dredge dish and leftover bread slices to one side.

Melt 2 tablespoons of butter in a large saucepan. Add apples, lemon zest, lemon juice and cloves, and cook gently until the apples are soft but not mushy. Continue to cook the apples, uncovered, until they are quite dry. Stir in sugar to taste.

Add bread crumbs to the apple mixture, then pile the apple mixture into the bread-lined baking dish. Cover the apple mixture with the remaining slices of buttered and sugared bread.

Cover the baking dish with foil (or a lid) and bake for 45-50 minutes.

Unmold onto a serving dish and serve hot.

Makes 6-8 servings.

Scottish Plum Crumble

1½ lbs. ripe plums
¾ cup brown sugar, firmly packed
1 cup flour
⅔ cup rolled oats
½ teaspoon ground cinnamon
6 tablespoons butter or margarine, softened

Preheat oven to 350° F.

Wash the plums, cut them in half and remove the stones. Mix the fruit with ½ cup of sugar. Place the fruit and sugar mixture into a 1-quart baking dish and set aside.

In a mixing bowl, sift together the flour and cinnamon. Add the oats and mix thoroughly.

Using a pastry blender or two knives, cut in the butter into the dry ingredients until the butter is evenly distributed. Knead the mixture with your hands if necessary to make sure the ingredients are thoroughly combined. Add the remaining sugar and mix well.

Spread the crumble mixture evenly over the plums, completely covering the fruit. Bake for 45-50 minutes or until the topping is golden brown and the fruit is cooked.

Makes 6-8 servings. Serve hot with *Custard Sauce* (also in this cookbook!).

Variations: Use two 29-oz. cans of whole plums, drained and pitted, in place of the fresh plums. You may wish to use less sugar with canned plums.

Cranberry Delight

1 cup graham cracker crumbs
¼ cup butter or margarine, melted
1 can whole cranberry sauce
¼ cup chopped nuts
1 8-oz. package cream cheese, softened
⅓ cup powdered sugar
1 tablespoon milk
1 teaspoon vanilla
1 cup whipped cream or whipped topping*

In a large mixing bowl, combine the graham cracker crumbs and melted butter. Press firmly and evenly onto the bottom of an 8-inch square pan.

In another mixing bowl, combine softened cream cheese, powdered sugar, milk and vanilla, mixing until well blended. Fold in the whipped cream or topping*, then spoon the mixture into the crust.

Mix together the cranberry sauce and nuts. Spoon this over the top of the cream cheese layer. Chill several hours or overnight.

Makes 8 tangy, tasty servings.

*If you use frozen whipped topping for this recipe, have it thawed ahead of time *before* folding it into the cream cheese mixture.

Strawberry Rhubarb Slump

Refreshing summertime goodness

TOPPING:
1 cup flour
¼ cup sugar
1 teaspoon baking powder
¼ teaspoon baking soda
A dash of salt
¼ cup butter or margarine
6 tablespoons buttermilk
  or sour milk

FRUIT:
3 cups whole strawberries, hulled
3 cups sliced rhubarb
½ cup sugar
½ cup water
1 tablespoon cornstarch

Prepare the topping: In a large mixing bowl, combine the flour, sugar, baking powder, baking soda, and salt. Cut in the butter with a pastry blender or 2 knives until the mixture is crumbly. Make a well in the center of the dry ingredients and pour in the buttermilk. Stir until the dry ingredients are just moistened; be careful not to over-mix.

Prepare the fruit: In a large skillet, combine the strawberries, rhubarb, sugar and water. Cover and cook over medium heat 10 minutes, stirring occasionally. In a small dish, mix the cornstarch with a little cold water and add it to the fruit mixture. Bring to a boil; once boiling, cook 1 minute or until thickened, stirring constantly.

Drop heaping tablespoonfuls of the topping onto the hot fruit mixture. Lower the heat, cover, and cook for 10 minutes. Remove from heat and allow to cool.

Makes 6-8 servings. Best served warm — great with ice cream!

Slump is an old-fashioned term referring to a cobbler-like dessert which is cooked on top of the stove rather than baked. The name probably derives from the observation that the dessert slumps in the dish when served.

Fabulous Fruit Salad

1 cup orange juice
1 cup water
½ cup sugar
½ teaspoon ground cinnamon
2 tangerines or oranges
2 peaches
1 cup strawberries or raspberries
¼ cup blanched, chopped almonds

In a saucepan over medium heat, combine the orange juice, water, sugar, and cinnamon. Cook the mixture, stirring occasionally, until the liquid turns into a syrup and has boiled down to about half it's original amount. (This should take about 45 minutes.) Allow the syrup to cool.

Peel, seed, and segment the oranges, cutting away any white membrane. Peel the peaches,* then cut the peaches and strawberries into bite-size pieces.

Combine all fruit in a serving bowl and pour the syrup over them. Chill thoroughly (about 1 hour). Sprinkle with chopped almonds and serve.

Serves 6. If you prefer, you may add or substitute other fresh fruits for the fruits noted above: canteloupe, melon, nectarines, apricots, and kiwi are all good choices, when in season.

*Note: Peaches are *much* easier to peel if they are speared on a fork and dipped into a pan of boiling water for a few seconds. Don't cook the peach in the process, however; a few seconds is all it takes!

Fruit Foole

In Shakespeare's time, to call someone a "foole"
was a term of endearment!

2 cups whipped cream
2 cups chopped peeled fruit — apricots,
   peaches, apples, pears, plums...
¼ cup sugar, or to taste

Place any kind of fruit you like into a saucepan and add the sugar. Cook over low heat until the fruit is soft. Transfer the fruit to a blender and puree the fruit until it is liquid.

Gently fold the pureed sweetened fruit into the whipped topping. Refrigerate or freeze for several hours before serving. The result is a sweet, fluffy taste sensation!

This is one of the all-time simplest desserts — and oddly enough, one of the oldest recorded desserts, as well!

Don't be foole-ed: there's more on the next page!

FOOLE-ISH VARIATIONS:

• If you wish, you may substitute 1 package (1.5 oz.) of prepared whipped topping mix or 2 cups of frozen whipped topping for the whipped cream. Omit the sugar if using this substitution.

• Gooseberries or blueberries can also be used for Foole. Mash the berries together with sugar in a saucepan. Cook until soft, then push the mixture through a sieve to remove the seeds and skins.

• Raspberries do not require cooking. Puree the raspberries in a blender, then strain out the seeds by pushing the puree through a finely-meshed sieve. Add sugar and fold into whipped cream.

SUPERQUICK FOOLE:

• 1 cup of your favorite jam or fruit spread, pureed in a blender, or 1 cup of sweetened apple sauce, can be substituted for the cooked, pureed fruit and sugar. Remember that if you use this variation with prepared whipped topping, the foole may come out extra-sweet.

Baked Bananas

4 medium-sized bananas
¼ cup brown sugar, firmly packed into cup
1½ teaspoons lemon juice
½ teaspoon ground cinnamon
1 teaspoon rum flavoring
2 tablespoons butter or margarine, melted

Preheat oven to 350° F. (325° if you are using a glass pan). Grease an 8-inch baking dish.
Peel the bananas and cut in half lengthwise. Place the sliced bananas in the baking dish, cut-side down.
In a small mixing bowl, combine all of the remaining ingredients. Sprinkle evenly over the bananas.
Bake for 15 minutes. Serve warm and gooey.

ADDITIVES:

If you wish, you can place 2 tablespoons of any flavored jam on top of the baked bananas for a split-like treat!

Pineapple Upside-Down Cake

2 tablespoons butter or margarine
¼ cup brown sugar, firmly packed
1 8¼-oz. can sliced or chunked pineapple,
   drained (save the juice)
2 eggs
¾ cup granulated sugar
½ cup reserved pineapple juice
1 teaspoon vanilla extract
1¼ cups flour
1 teaspoon baking powder
½ teaspoon salt

Heat oven to 350° F. (325° F. for a glass pan). Place the butter in an 8-inch round or square baking pan. Set the pan in the oven and allow the butter to melt. Remove the pan from the oven and sprinkle the brown sugar evenly over the melted butter. Arrange the pineapple slices or chunks over the sugar mixture in the pan.

In a mixing bowl, add the eggs and beat them for 3 to 5 minutes until they are light and thick. Gradually beat in the granulated sugar. Add the reserved pineapple juice and vanilla extract. Add the flour, baking powder, and salt into the egg mixture and mix thoroughly until the batter is smooth. Pour the batter over the pineapple in the baking pan. Bake about 40 minutes, or until a pick inserted in the center of the cake comes out clean.

Remove the cake from the oven and it (still in the pan) on a wire rack. Allow the cake to cool for 5 minutes in the pan, then invert it onto a serving dish.

Makes 8 servings. Best served warm.

For a colorful touch, try adding a few drained maraschino cherries to the pineapple slices or chunks!

Tropical Bake

4 teaspoons flour
1 tablespoon cold water
1 20-oz. can pineapple, with juice
3 bananas
1 teaspoon lemon juice
½ cup flaked coconut or chopped nuts
½ teaspoon ground nutmeg
1 tablespoon bread crumbs or wheat germ

Preheat oven to 350° F. (or 325° F. if using a glass pan). Grease an 8-inch square baking pan and set aside.

Mix flour and water in a small bowl. In a medium saucepan, combine the flour mixture with the pineapple and juice. Bring to a boil over medium heat, stirring often as the mixture thickens. Remove from heat and set aside.

Peel the bananas and cut them into ½-inch slices. Line the prepared baking dish with the banana slices. Sprinkle bananas with coconut (or nuts), lemon juice, and nutmeg. Pour the hot pineapple mixture evenly over all, and sprinkle with bread crumbs. Bake for 15 minutes.

Berry Kutchen

½ cup butter or margarine
⅓ cup sugar
½ teaspoon vanilla
1 egg
Pinch of salt
1 teaspoon grated lemon peel
1 tablespoon sour cream
1¾ cup flour
1 teaspoon baking powder
2 cups berries, any kind

STREUSEL TOPPING:

¼ cup butter or margarine
¾ cup flour
⅓ cup sugar
½ teaspoon ground cinnamon

Preheat oven to 375° F . (350° F . if you are using a glass pan). Grease an 8-inch round cake pan and set aside.

Wash the berries, drain them well, and set aside.

In a large mixing bowl, cream the butter with the sugar and vanilla, using a spoon or electric mixer. Mix in the egg, salt, lemon peel, and sour cream.

In a separate bowl, mix the flour and baking powder using a spoon or wire whisk. Add the flour mixture to the creamed mixture and mix thoroughly.

Spread the dough into the prepared pan, pressing a little up the side. Liberally spread the berries over the dough. If the berries are sour (as opposed to just tart), sprinkle them lightly with sugar.

For the streusel topping, place the butter in a small mixing bowl. Cream together with flour, sugar and cinnamon. Sprinkle this mixture over the berries. Bake for 30-45 minutes.

Makes 6-8 servings. Serve topped with whipped topping or whipped cream.

Apple Yum!

1 cup flour
1 teaspoon baking powder
1 teaspoon ground cinnamon
⅓ cup butter or margarine, softened
½ cup packed brown sugar
1 egg
¼ cup milk
½ cup shredded sharp cheddar cheese
3 apples, peeled, cored, and cut into slices
   (about 3½ cups slices)
½ cup white sugar
½ cup chopped nuts

Preheat oven to 375° F. (350° F. for a glass pan). Grease an 8-inch baking dish and set aside.

In a small bowl, combine the flour, baking powder and ½ teaspoon of the cinnamon. In a separate larger bowl, cream together the butter and brown sugar until well mixed. Add the egg to the butter mixture and beat well. Add a portion of the dry ingredients to the creamed mixture, alternately adding milk and mixing well after each addition. Pour the finished batter into prepared pan.

Sprinkle chopped nuts over the batter. Layer the apples over the nuts, and sprinkle the apples with white sugar and the remaining cinnamon. Bake for 35 minutes.

Sprinkle grated cheese over the top of the dessert as soon as it comes out of the oven, and allow the cheese to melt.

Makes 6 to 8 servings. For an extra-sweet variation, serve *Apple Yum!* with whipped cream.

Strawberry Shortcake

A refreshing summertime treat

1½ lbs. fresh strawberries
2 tablespoons sugar, more or less
2 cups flour
1 tablespoon baking powder
½ teaspoon salt
½ cup butter or margarine
1 egg
¾ cup light cream or evaporated milk

Wash the strawberries, remove the stems, and slice them into a bowl. Add 2 tablespoons of sugar and mash the combination with a fork, breaking the strawberries into pieces. Add more sugar if needed, according to taste. Allow the mix to sit for about 30 minutes.

Preheat oven to 450° F. (425° F. if using a glass pan). Grease an 8-inch round cake pan and set aside.

In a mixing bowl, mix together the flour, sugar, baking powder, and salt, using a spoon or wire whisk. Cut in the butter with a pastry blender or two knives until the mixture resembles coarse crumbs. Make a well in the center of the dry ingredients.

In a separate bowl, beat the egg; then mix in the light cream or evaporated milk. Pour the mix all at once into the center of the dry ingredients. Stir together until the dry ingredients are just moistened. Spread the dough into the prepared pan, building up the edges of the dough slightly so that the shortcake will bake with a flattened top.

Bake for 15 to 18 minutes, or until a toothpick inserted in the center comes out clean. Remove the shortcake from the pan and let it cool on a wire rack for 5 minutes.

Place shortcake on a serving plate, or divide between 6 to 8 individual dessert plates or bowls. Spoon the prepared strawberries over shortcake.

Makes 6-8 servings. Serve with your choice of whipped toppings, or with ice cream — or with nothing! Great either warm or chilled.

Peach Crisp

Simple and sweet

4 cups fresh peaches, peeled and sliced
  (or 2 cans, drained)
2 tablespoons lemon juice
1 cup flour
½ cup packed brown sugar
¼ cup butter or margarine, softened
½ teaspoon salt
1 teaspoon ground cinnamon

Preheat oven to 375° F. (350° F. if using a glass pan). Lightly grease an 8-inch baking pan. Place sliced peaches in the dish and sprinkle with lemon juice.

In a mixing bowl, combine the flour, brown sugar, salt, and cinnamon. Cut in the butter using a pastry blender or two knives, or use your fingertips to work the ingredients together until the mixture is crumbly. Spread this over the peaches in the baking dish.

Bake for 30 minutes, until the top is nicely browned.

Makes 4-6 quick and tasty servings. Serve hot or cold!

Apples and Dumplings

2 tart apples — peeled, cored,
   and sliced thick
½ cup chopped nuts (optional)

SYRUP:
2 cups cold water
1 tablespoon corn starch
¾ cup brown sugar
½ teaspoon ground cinnamon

DUMPLINGS:
1½ cups flour
1 tablespoon sugar
1 tablespoon baking powder
½ teaspoon salt
¼ cup butter or margarine
¾ cup milk

In a medium-sized saucepan, combine cold water and cornstarch. Add brown sugar and cinnamon, and mix thoroughly.

Bring the mixture to a boil over medium heat, stirring constantly, then lower the heat and allow the mixture to simmer. Stir occasionally until a syrup is formed. Add apple slices to the syrup and bring to a boil.

Make dumplings: in a large mixing bowl, stir together the flour, sugar, baking powder and salt. Cut in butter with a pastry blender or two knives until the mixture is crumbly. Make a well in the center of the flour mixture.

Pour the milk into the center of the dry ingredients, and stir until the flour mixture is just moistened.

Drop the dumpling dough by tablespoonfuls into the boiling syrup mixture, and sprinkle with nuts. Cover the boiling mixture and simmer for 15 to 20 minutes without peeking. Serve immediately.

Makes 6 piping-hot servings.

Cookies!

Scotch Shortbread

A favorite of the Highlands

2 cups flour
1 cup butter or margarine, softened
¾ cup powdered sugar, sifted
½ teaspoon baking powder
⅛ teaspoon salt

Preheat oven to 325° F. (300° F. if you are using a glass pan). Measure all ingredients into a large bowl. Knead the ingredients by hand until everything is well-blended. (The dough will be soft.) Pat the dough evenly into an 8-inch square or round baking pan. Prick the top of the dough all over with fork.

Bake the shortbread about 45 minutes or until golden.

While the shortbread is still warm, cut into 12 wedges with a knife. (Cut into squares if baked in a square pan.) Let the shortbread cool in pan on wire rack. Once removed from the pan, store the cookies in a tightly covered container.

Oatmeal Cookies

Old-fashioned goodness for every age

1 cup flour

1 teaspoon salt

½ teaspoon baking soda

¾ cup shortening, softened

¾ cup brown sugar, firmly packed

⅓ cup granulated sugar

1 egg

¼ cup water

1 teaspoon vanilla extract

3 cups rolled oats, uncooked

½ to 1 cup chocolate chips, chopped nuts,
  and/or raisins (optional)

Preheat oven to 350° F. Grease a standard-sized cookie sheet, and set aside.

In a small mixing bowl, sift together the flour, salt, and baking soda. In a large mixing bowl, add shortening, sugar, brown sugar, egg, water and vanilla, and beat until creamy. Add the flour mixture to the creamed mixture and blend well.

Stir in the rolled oats (plus any optional ingredients, if you wish).

Drop the cookie dough by teaspoonfuls onto the greased cookie sheet. Bake for 9 - 10 minutes, or until the edges are golden and the tops of the cookies are starting to look dry. Remove cookies to a wire rack to cool.

The dough for any 'drop' cookie (like Oatmeal Cookies, where the dough is dropped onto the cookie sheet) can be mixed up ahead of time and chilled until ready to use. If chilled dough is used for a drop cookie, the cookie may "melt" less over the sheet while baking, so the baked cookie will be thicker. Chilled drop-cookie dough may also require an extra minute or two of baking time.

Peanut Butter Cookies

Yet another delicious tradition!

1½ cups flour
1 teaspoon baking soda
½ teaspoon salt
½ cup shortening
⅓ cup peanut butter
½ cup granulated sugar
½ cup brown sugar,
    firmly packed
1 egg
½ teaspoon vanilla extract

Preheat oven to 350° F. Grease a standard cookie sheet and set to one side.

In a small mixing bowl, stir together the flour, baking soda, and salt. In a large mixing bowl, add shortening, peanut butter, sugar and brown sugar, and beat until well blended. Add the egg and vanilla, and beat the mixture until it is light and fluffy.

Add the dry ingredients to the fluffy batter, and blend thoroughly to make a stiff dough.

Using your hands, shape the dough into balls, using about 1 tablespoon of dough for each ball. Place the dough ball on the greased cookie sheet, and flatten it gently with a fork.

Bake the cookies for 12 minutes. Remove immediately to wire racks to cool.

VARIATIONS:

• Try adding ½ cup chocolate (or other flavor) chips, or ½ cup chopped nuts to the dough.

• For a 'healthier' (tasting) cookie, try substituting half of the white flour with whole wheat flour.

Bizchocitos

Serve this South-of-the-Border treat with some Fiesta Hot Chocolate *(also in this book)!*

COOKIE DOUGH

3 cups flour
1½ teaspoons baking powder
½ teaspoon salt
1 cup lard or shortening,
  softened
½ cup sugar
½ teaspoon anise seed
1 egg, well beaten
2 tablespoons water

TOPPING

½ teaspoon ground cinnamon
¼ cup sugar

In a small mixing bowl, mix together the flour, baking powder, and salt; set aside. In a separate larger mixing bowl, cream the lard (or shortening) thoroughly. Add sugar and anise seed and mix in. Add eggs, and beat until the mixture is light and fluffy. Add the flour mixture to the fluffy batter and mix thoroughly. Add water and knead the dough with your hands until all ingredients are well mixed. Cover the dough and chill for several hours until firm.

Preheat oven to 350° F. Grease a standard cookie sheet and set aside.

In a small bowl, mix the sugar and cinnamon together.

Remove about ¼ of the cookie dough from the refrigerator. (Leave the rest refrigerated while you work.) Place the dough on a well-floured board, and sprinkle a tiny amount of flour across the top of the dough and across a rolling pin. Roll out the cookie dough until it is about ¼ inch thick, rolling in short strokes outward from the center of the dough. Avoid working excess flour into the dough.

With floured cookie cutters, cut the cookie dough into desired shapes, pressing straight down with the cutter. Using a floured spatula, move the cut-out cookies to the greased cookie sheet. Repeat this process with the remaining cookie dough, using only a small amount of dough at a time.

Sprinkle the top of the cookies with the cinnamon/sugar mixture. Bake 8-10 minutes or until lightly brown. Remove the cookies to a wire rack and allow to cool.

Nankhatai

These go great with Classi Lassi *or* East Indian Tea

1 cup whole wheat flour
¼ teaspoon baking powder
½ teaspoon ground cardamom
3 tablespoons butter or margarine, softened
½ cup brown sugar
Halved pistachios or blanched almonds for garnish

Preheat oven to 325° F.

In a small mixing bowl, stir together the flour, baking powder and cardamom. In a separate bowl, cream together the butter, and sugar. Add the flour mixture, and knead well with floured hands.

Pinch off lumps of dough and form into balls about 1 inch in diameter. Place the balls of dough onto a greased baking sheet and flatten slightly, using the bottom of a glass that has been dipped in whole wheat flour. Press half a nut into the center of each cookie.

Bake cookies for 20-25 minutes, or until lightly browned. Remove the cookies to a wire rack and allow to cool. Store the finished cookies in an airtight tin.

Sesame Cookies

2 cups flour
¾ teaspoon baking powder
½ cup sugar
½ cup shortening, melted but not hot
1 egg, beaten
2 tablespoons ice water
1 egg yolk for glazing
¾ cup sesame seeds for topping

Sift the flour, baking powder, and sugar into a bowl and combine. Make a well in the center of the dry ingredients and pour in the melted (*not* hot) shortening. Add the egg and ice water. Work the flour mixture into the liquid ingredients until a smooth ball of dough is formed, using your hands if necessary to combine ingredients thoroughly. Chill the dough until it is firm.

Preheat oven to 375° F. Work with small portions of dough at a time (keeping the rest refrigerated). Roll the dough out ⅛ inch thick onto a lightly floured surface. Cut the dough into circles with a floured cookie cutter, and arrange on a greased baking sheet. Brush with egg yolk and sprinkle with the sesame seeds. Bake 12 minutes or until browned.

Nane Shirini

From the exotic lands of the Middle East

1 cup flour
½ teaspoon baking powder
½ cup vegetable shortening
½ cup sugar
1 egg yolk
½ teaspoon vanilla extract
½ teaspoon almond extract
½ teaspoon lemon extract

Preheat oven to 300° F. In a large mixing bowl, sift the flour and baking powder together. In a separate bowl, cream the shortening and granulated sugar thoroughly, then blend in the egg yolk and flavored extracts; mix well. Gradually add the dry ingredients and mix thoroughly until the dough is well blended.

Scoop small lumps of dough with a teaspoon and, using your hands, roll the dough into round balls about 1 inch in diameter. Place the dough balls on an ungreased cookie sheet and flatten them slightly with a spoon. Prick some of the cookies with the tines of a fork to give a little variety in appearance, if desired.

Bake for about 20 minutes or until lightly browned.

Nut & Spice Cookies

2 cups flour
1 tablespoon baking soda
¾ teaspoon ground ginger
¾ teaspoon ground cinnamon
¾ teaspoon ground cloves
¼ teaspoon salt
¾ cup shortening
½ cup granulated sugar
½ cup firmly packed brown sugar
1 egg
¼ cup molasses
2 cups chopped walnuts or other nuts
Granulated sugar for coating

Preheat oven to 350° F. In a small mixing bowl, stir together the flour, soda, spices and salt. In a separate larger bowl, cream together the shortening, sugars, and egg, mixing until they are light and fluffy. Stir in molasses, then add the flour mixture and the walnuts.

Place sugar for coating in a small dish. Scoop out lumps of dough with a tablespoon and, using your hands, shape the dough into balls about 1½ inches in diameter. Roll the dough in the sugar to coat each ball thoroughly.

Place balls of sugared cookie dough about 6 inches apart on well-greased baking sheets. Flatten the dough into circles, using the bottom of a glass that has been dipped in sugar.

Bake for 10-12 minutes, or until the tops of the cookies spring back when touched lightly. Remove the cookies from the oven and allow to cool slightly on baking sheet; then, using a broad spatula, remove the cookies to a wire rack to cool completely.

COOKIE HINTS

If you are making several batches of cookies and have a limited number of baking sheets, allow the baking sheets to cool before using them for a fresh batch of dough. A hot cookie sheet can cause the bottom of your cookie to overbake.

Cherry-Nut Puffs

A low-fat delight

1 egg white (at room temperature)
½ teaspoon vinegar
½ teaspoon vanilla
⅛ teaspoon salt
1 cup powdered sugar, sifted
¼ cup finely chopped pecans or other nuts
2 tablespoons finely chopped maraschino cherries

Preheat oven to 300° F. Place the egg white in a large mixing bowl (preferably glass or metal), and beat with an electric mixer until frothy. Add vinegar, vanilla and salt, and continue beating until soft peaks form when the beaters are lifted. Gradually add powdered sugar a little at a time, beating after each addition; do *not* add the sugar at once! Continue beating until stiff peaks form when the beaters are lifted. The mixture should be stiff and glossy.

Gently fold the pecans and cherries into the fluff.

Drop by teaspoonfuls 2 inches apart onto a well-greased cookie sheets. Bake 18-20 minutes or until cookies are firm.

Mint Puffs

Light as a cloud and low-fat, too!

1 egg white (at room temperature)
¼ teaspoon salt
½ teaspoon vanilla extract
Dash cream of tartar
⅓ cup sugar
¼ teaspoon mint extract

Preheat oven to 350° F. In a large mixing bowl (preferably glass or metal), place egg whites, salt, vanilla extract and cream of tartar. Beat with an electric mixer until soft peaks form when the beaters are lifted (about 4 minutes). Gradually add sugar and beat it into the fluff, adding only a little at a time; do not add all the sugar at once. When the meringue appears glossy and forms stiff peaks when the beaters are lifted, beat in mint extract.

Drop the fluff by teaspoonfuls onto a lightly greased cookie sheet. Baked for 20 minutes or until golden brown on bottom.

Carefully remove the fragile cookies from the baking sheet and allow to cool on a wire rack.

Campout Bars

S'more flavors baked in a cookie!

½ cup butter or margarine, softened
¾ cup sugar
1 egg
1 teaspoon vanilla extract
1⅓ cup flour
¾ cup graham cracker crumbs
1 teaspoon baking powder
¼ teaspoon salt
1 cup milk chocolate or semi-sweet
   chocolate chips
1 cup marshmallow creme

Heat oven to 350° F. (325° F. for a glass pan). Grease an 8-inch square baking pan and set aside.

In a mixing bowl, stir together the flour, graham cracker crumbs, baking powder and salt. In a separate large mixing bowl, add butter and sugar and beat with an electric mixer until the mixture is light and fluffy. Add egg and vanilla, and beat well.

Add the flour mixture to butter mixture, beating until blended.

Press half of dough into the prepared pan. Arrange chocolate chips or pieces of chocolate bars over the dough. Spread marshmallow creme over the dough and chocolate. Drop bits of remaining dough onto the marshmallow layer, and gently press the dough into the marshmallow.

Bake 30-35 minutes, or until lightly browned. Cool completely in pan on wire rack. Cut into bars or squares.

Substitution: 1 cup miniature marshmallows, or 8 large marshmallows snipped down to small pieces, can be used in place of the marshmallow creme. This will not make as neat-looking a bar as using marshmallow creme, but it will still taste great.

Granola Bars

Great for snacking while backpacking!

2 cups oatmeal, uncooked

⅔ cup shredded coconut

½ cup raisins, chopped dates, figs, currants, or any chopped dried fruit

½ cup chopped peanuts or other nuts

⅓ cup packed brown sugar

⅓ cup wheat germ

¼ cup flour

½ cup butter or margarine, melted but not hot

1 egg

2 tablespoons honey

1 teaspoon vanilla

½ cup chocolate chips (optional)

Preheat oven to 350° F. (325° F. for a glass pan). Grease a 13x9-inch baking pan and set aside.

In a large mixing bowl, combine oats, coconut, raisins, peanuts, sugar, wheat germ, and flour. In a separate smaller bowl, mix together the melted margarine, egg, honey and vanilla. Combine the liquid ingredients with the dry ingredients, using your hands if necessary to thoroughly combine ingredients. Press the mixture firmly into the prepared pan.

Bake 25 minutes. Let cool, then cut into bars. Nutty-grainy fun!

Nanaimo Bars

A Canadian specialty

LAYER 1

½ cup butter or margarine
¼ cup sugar
1 egg
4 tablespoons unsweetened cocoa, sifted
2 cups graham cracker crumbs
1 cup flaked coconut
½ cup chopped nuts

LAYER 2

¼ cup butter or margarine
3 tablespoons milk
2 tablespoons dry vanilla pudding mix
2 cups sifted powdered sugar

LAYER 3

⅔ cup semi-sweet chocolate chips
1 teaspoon butter or margarine

In a double boiler, mix ½ cup of butter, the sugar, egg, and cocoa. Cook over boiling water, stirring continuously, until the mixture resembles pudding.

In a large mixing bowl, combine the graham cracker crumbs, coconut, and nuts. Add this to the cooked mixture, blending thoroughly. Let the mixture cool, but not harden. Spread and press the combined ingredients into an 8-inch square pan.

In a glass or metal mixing bowl, cream together ¼ cup of butter, the powdered sugar, and the pudding mix. Add the milk and mix thoroughly. Spread this mixture over the first layer in the pan.

Melt the semi-sweet chocolate over hot water or in the microwave. Add the butter and blend well. Spread over the second layer.

Let set until firm, then chill and keep refrigerated. Cut into bars with a warm knife, dipping the knife in water every few cuts to keep it from sticking to the bars. Serve the bars cold.

Lemon Bars

Light, tangy and refreshing

1 cup flour
⅓ cup powdered sugar, sifted
½ cup butter or margarine
4 eggs
¾ cup sugar
½ cup lemon juice
1 tablespoon powdered sugar
   for topping

Preheat oven to 350° F. (325° F. for a glass pan).

In a medium-sized mixing bowl, combine the flour and ⅓ cup powdered sugar. With a pastry cutter or two knives, cut in the butter until the mixture resembles small peas; the mixture will be dry and crumbly. Press the mix into the bottom of an ungreased 8-inch square baking pan. Bake 15 minutes or until lightly golden.

Place the eggs in a medium-sized mixing bowl, and beat until they are pale and thickened (about 3 minutes using an electric mixer). Gradually add granulated sugar and continue beating 1 minute longer, or until the mixture is thick. Add the lemon juice and mix thoroughly.

Pour the liquid into the hot crust. Bake 15 minutes or until golden, or when a toothpick inserted in the center comes out clean.

With a sifter, sprinkle 1 tablespoon of powdered sugar over the top of the uncut bars. Let them cool in the pan atop a wire rack.

Cut into squares, and serve at room temperature.

Peanut Cookies (Kulikuli)

1¼ cups flour
½ teaspoon salt
½ teaspoon baking powder
¼ cup butter or margarine, softened
⅔ cup sugar
1 egg
1 teaspoon vanilla extract
½ cup very finely chopped peanuts

In a mixing bowl, sift together the flour, salt, and baking powder. In a separate larger bowl, cream the butter until soft. Gradually add the sugar, mixing well. Add the egg and vanilla extract, and mix again.

Add the flour mixture to the butter mixture a little at a time, mixing thoroughly after each addition. Add chopped peanuts and mix again. Place the bowl of dough in the refrigerator to chill for 1 hour.

Heat oven to 350° F. Grease cookie sheets and set aside.

With lightly floured hands, roll teaspoonfuls of the dough into balls. Place the balls of dough on the greased cookie sheets and flatten them into a patty, using the bottom of a glass that has been dipped in flour.

Bake 12-15 minutes. Remove the cookies from the baking sheets with a spatula and transfer to a wire rack to cool.

Coconut Macaroons

1 egg white (at room temperature)
6 tablespoons granulated sugar
1 cup flaked coconut
Powdered sugar, sifted
Granulated sugar

Preheat oven to 325° F. Grease cookie sheets and set aside.

Put the egg white in a mixing bowl and beat with an egg beater (or electric mixer) until it forms soft peaks when the beater is lifted. Gradually add 6 tablespoons sugar a little at a time, beating each time; do not add all the sugar at once. Use a spoon to gently fold in the coconut.

Dust your hands with the powdered sugar. Scoop small lumps of dough with a teaspoon and roll them between the palms of your hands to make 1-inch balls. Arrange balls of dough on greased baking sheets. Sprinkle a little granulated sugar over each cookie.

Bake 16-18 minutes or until lightly browned. Don't bake the cookies too long; these cookies should be a little soft on the inside.

Remove from oven, and transfer to a wire rack to cool.

Chinese Almond Cookies

½ cup brown sugar, firmly packed into cup
½ cup butter or margarine, softened
1¼ cups flour
¾ cup finely chopped blanched almonds
24 - 30 whole blanched toasted almonds (for garnish)

Preheat oven to 325°. In a mixing bowl, cream together the brown sugar and butter. Stir in the flour. Add chopped almonds and mix well.

Shape the dough into balls about 1½ inches in diameter. The dough will be sticky; if needed, sprinkle a little flour on your hands to make the dough easier to handle. Place balls of dough on an ungreased cookie sheets about 2 inches apart. Dip the bottom of a drinking glass in flour, and flatten the balls until they are ½ inch thick. Press a single blanched almond into the top of each cookie.

Bake the cookies for 15 minutes or until they are golden brown. Allow the cookies to cool on the cookie sheet for 2 minutes, then carefully move them to wire racks to cool completely.

Apricot Oatmeal Bars

CRUMB MIXTURE

¾ cup flour
¾ cup rolled oats
¼ cup sugar
6 tablespoons butter or margarine, melted
¼ teaspoon baking soda
Dash salt
1 teaspoon vanilla extract

FILLING:

5 oz. apricot preserves
2 tablespoons flaked coconut (optional)

Heat oven to 350° F. (325° F. for a glass pan). Grease a 8-inch square baking pan and set aside.

In a large mixing bowl, combine all crumb mixture ingredients. Beat until the mixture is crumbly, scraping the sides of the bowl often.

Set aside ¾ cup of the crumb mixture. Press the remaining crumb mixture into the prepared baking pan.

Spread apricot preserves to within ½ inch of the edge of the crumb mixture. Sprinkle the reserved crumb mixture over the top, then sprinkle the top with coconut.

Bake for 22-27 minutes, or until the edges are lightly browned. Cool completely on wire racks.

Cut into bars, and serve at room temperature.

Rag Doll Bars

Irresistible!

LAYER 1
¼ cup butter or margarine, softened
½ cup brown sugar
¼ teaspoon salt
1 cup flour

LAYER 2
2 eggs
1 cup brown sugar, firmly packed
¼ teaspoon salt
1 teaspoon vanilla extract
1 cup crisped rice cereal
½ cup chopped nuts
1 cup flaked coconut

Preheat oven to 350° F. (325° F. for a glass pan). Grease an 8-inch square pan and set aside.

In a small mixing bowl, mix together the flour and salt.

In a large mixing bowl, cream together the butter and the sugar until the mixture is light and fluffy.

Add the flour mixture, cutting it into the creamed mixture with a pastry cutter or two knives until the combination is crumbly. Press this mixture into the prepared pan.

Bake for 15 minutes, or until lightly golden.

In a glass or metal mixing bowl, beat the eggs until they are fluffy. Add brown sugar, salt, vanilla extract, cereal, nuts, and coconut, and mix thoroughly. Spread this mixture over the baked layer.

Bake for an additional 12 minutes, then allow to cool.

Cut into squares. If you wish, frost or sprinkle with powdered sugar. Store the finished cookies in the refrigerator.

Miscellaneous Favorites

Scottish Tablet

A fudgy favorite from the Highlands

2¼ cups sugar
1 cup + 2 tablespoons cream or evaporated milk
Pinch of cream of tartar
½ cup finely chopped nuts (optional)
Your choice of flavorings:
  • 1 teaspoon vanilla extract; or
  • 1 tablespoon instant coffee dissolved in
    ¼ cup hot water

Butter an 8-inch pan and set aside.
Combine sugar and cream in a large saucepan. Over low heat, stir the cream and sugar constantly with a wooden spoon until no particles of sugar are left and the mixture is smooth. (If sugar crystals form on the insides of the pan while stirring, use a pastry brush or a clean cloth dipped in cold water to brush them off.)
When the sugar has completely dissolved, continue stirring

and *slowly* bring the mixture to a gentle boil. Once the mixture is boiling, stir in the cream of tartar.

Clip a candy thermometer to the side of the pan, taking care that the thermometer bulb does not rest on the bottom of the pan. Allow the mixture to simmer gently without stirring. Continue slowly cooking candy until the thermometer reaches 240° F. (soft ball stage*).

Remove the pan from the heat. Stir in any nuts and your choice of flavorings. Begin beating the cooling mixture with a wooden spoon for about 5 minutes, until the mixture starts to "grain" slightly and drops appear to be taking on a solid form. Quickly pour into the buttered pan.

Score with a knife into pieces and let set until cool.

* - If you do not have a candy thermometer, test to see if the candy has cooked long enough by dropping a tiny amount of the cooked mixture into a glass of very cold water. When the mixture hold its shape in the water and forms a soft lump (the 'soft ball' stage), it is ready.

Custard

2 cups milk	¼ teaspoon salt
3 eggs	1 ½ teaspoon vanilla
¼ cup sugar	Nutmeg

Preheat the oven to 350° F. and place 4 custard cups in a baking pan.

Put milk in a saucepan and "scald" the milk by heating it over low heat, just until tiny bubbles form around the edge of the pan. Do not boil the milk.

In a mixing bowl or pitcher, beat the eggs with a wire whisk until they are well blended. Stir in sugar, salt, and vanilla. Add the scalded milk gradually, stirring the eggs constantly with the wire whisk as you pour. Pour the mixture through a sieve into the custard cups, dividing the mixture evenly. Sprinkle a little nutmeg over each cup.

Place the baking pan with the filled custard cups in the oven. Carefully fill the baking pan with hot water until the water level is about 1 inch up the sides of the custard cups. Bake 30 to 40 minutes, or until a knife inserted in the center of a custard comes out clean. Remove from heat immediately.

Serve warm or cold.

Turkish Delight

A classic confectionery temptation.

2 cups sugar
1 cup water
4 tablespoons powdered gelatin
1 tablespoon rose water mixed with ¼ cup water, or
  ½ cup any combination citrus juices
  (lemon, orange, lime)
1 cup finely chopped almonds or pistachios (optional)
Food coloring (optional)
½ cup powdered sugar
½ cup cornstarch

Lightly grease an 8x8-inch square pan and set aside.

In a heavy saucepan over medium heat, combine the sugar and ½ cup of the water. Bring the mixture to a boil and simmer 15 minutes, until sugar is completely dissolved and the mixture forms a syrup.

As the syrup is simmering, put the remaining ½ cup of water into a mixing bowl. Add the gelatin to the water and mix until the gelatin is thoroughly dissolved.

Add the dissolved gelatin to the simmering syrup. Clip a candy thermometer to the side of the pan, taking care that the thermometer bulb is not resting on the bottom of the pan. Continue simmering the syrup until the mixture reaches the soft-ball stage (about 240° F. on your candy thermometer.*)

Remove the syrup pan from the heat. Add your choice of flavorings to the syrup and stir gently. If you wish, add chopped nuts; food coloring may also be added at this point to tint the finished candy according to the type of flavor used.

Pour the mixture into the prepared pan. Let the candy chill until it is firm, about 24 hours.

In a wide, shallow bowl or plate, sift together the powdered sugar and cornstarch. With a lightly greased spatula, remove the chilled, firm candy from the pan and place on the powdered sugar. Then, using wet kitchen shears, cut the candy into cubes, about ½-inch square. Gently toss the candy in the powdered sugar until it is well coated. (If the candy should become too moist and absorb the powdered sugar, allow it to sit out on a plate, covered with a dry paper towel, until the candy is dry and less sticky. Recoat with additional powdered sugar.)

Pack your finished Turkish Delight in an airtight container, covering it with a little extra powdered sugar.

Quick Opera Fudge

2 packages regular vanilla pudding mix (not instant)
½ cup milk
½ teaspoon vanilla
½ cup butter or margarine
3½ cups powdered sugar, sifted
⅓ cup maraschino cherries, chopped
½ cup chopped walnuts
Walnut halves for garnish (optional)

Butter an 8x8-inch square pan and set aside.

Drain the maraschino cherries on paper towels and set aside.

In a large saucepan, melt butter. Stir in the dry pudding mixes and milk. Slowly cook the pudding mixture, stirring slowly until the mixture comes to a boil. Boil for one minute, stirring constantly, then remove from heat.

Stir the vanilla into the cooked mixture. Beat in powdered sugar until the mixture is smooth. Stir in walnuts and cherries.

Pat the mixture into the prepared pan. Once it is firm, score the candy into 1-inch squares. Garnish each square with a walnut half. Chill thoroughly and finish cutting candy into squares before serving.

Sponge Candy

1 cup sugar
1 cup dark corn syrup
1 tablespoon white vinegar
1 tablespoon baking soda

Butter an 8-inch square pan and set aside.

In a heavy saucepan, combine sugar, corn syrup and vinegar. Cook over medium-low heat, stirring constantly, until the sugar has dissolved. (If sugar crystals form on the insides of the pan while stirring, use a pastry brush or a clean cloth dipped in cold water to brush them off.)

Clip a candy thermometer to the side of the pan; take care that the thermometer bulb is not resting on the bottom of the pan. Cook the candy, without stirring, until the candy thermometer reaches 300° F.* (hard crack stage.)

Remove the candy from heat and stir in the baking soda. Pour into prepared pan. The mixture will bubble and spread by itself. Cool the candy in the pan on a wire rack.

Break the cooled candy into pieces. Sponge candy can be stored 2 to 3 weeks in a tightly covered container with foil or plastic wrap between layers.

IMPORTANT NOTE: If you use a glass pan for making candy, be sure to warm the pan first using hot running water, then dry the pan thoroughly. Hot candy syrup hitting a cold glass pan may crack the glass.

* - If you do not have a candy thermometer, test by dropping a small amount of the candy mixture into a cup of very cold water. When the syrup separates into hard, brittle threads, it is ready.

Pecan Pie

A rich Southern tradition made easy

1 unbaked pie crust or graham cracker crust
¼ cup butter or margarine
1 cup firmly packed brown sugar
3 eggs
½ cup light corn syrup or molasses
1½ cups broken pecans or walnuts
1 teaspoon vanilla extract
½ teaspoon salt

If you are using a pastry crust, preheat the oven to 450° F.; prick the pie crust with a fork in several places and then bake the crust by itself for 5-7 minutes. Remove from oven and allow the pie crust to cool. Reduce the oven heat to 375° F.

Cream together the butter and brown sugar. Beat in the eggs, one at a time, until they are thoroughly blended. Stir in the corn syrup (or molasses), pecans, vanilla flavoring, and salt. Fill the partially-baked and cooled pie shell.

If you are using a pastry crust, cut a strip of tin foil about 1½ inch wide and use it to cover the edge of the piecrust to prevent overbrowning. Bake the pie for 40 minutes, or until a knife inserted in the filling comes out clean. Serve this pie warm or cold.

Lemon Meringue Pie

PIE:

1 cup sugar

3 tablespoons corn starch

1½ cups cold water

3 egg yolks, slightly beaten

2 teaspoons grated lemon rind

6 tablespoons lemon juice

1 tablespoon margarine

1 unbaked pie crust
  or graham cracker crust

MERINGUE:

3 egg whites

⅓ cup sugar

* - *Weeping* is when a watery residue forms between the filling and the meringue. This can easily happen in hot, humid weather. Sealing the filling with meringue can help prevent this occurrence.

If you are using a pastry crust, prick the crust with a fork in several places and bake at 325° F. for 5 minutes (or until lightly browned).

In a 2-quart saucepan, add the sugar and cornstarch and mix thoroughly. Gradually stir in water until the mixture is smooth. Add egg yolks and mix. Bring this mixture to a boil over medium heat, stirring constantly, and boil for 1 minute. Remove from heat and stir in lemon rind, lemon juice and margarine. Let cool, then pour into the baked pastry shell.

Preheat oven to 350° F. Make the meringue by placing the egg whites in a mixing bowl (preferably a glass or metal mixing bowl) and beating them with an electric mixer or egg beater until the whites appear and foamy. Add sugar a little at a time, beating well after each addition; do not add all the sugar at once. Continue beating the meringue until stiff peaks form when the beaters are lifted.

Spread some meringue around the edge of the filling, making sure that the meringue touches the crust on all sides; then cover the center, piling meringue highest towards the middle. Be sure to seal the edges of the pastry well with the meringue to avoid 'weeping.'*

Bake 15 minutes, or until the meringue is lightly browned. Cool the pie at room temperature away from any drafts.

Makes 6-8 servings (or less if you really love lemon meringue pie). Excellent served warm or cold!

Pumpkin Pie

Even turkeys give thanks for this timeless treat

1 cup packed brown sugar
1 tablespoon flour
1¼ teaspoon ground cinnamon
½ teaspoon ground ginger
¼ teaspoon ground cloves
1 1-lb. can (2 cups) pumpkin
1 9-oz. can (1⅔ cups) evaporated milk
1 egg, slightly beaten
2 unbaked pie crusts or graham cracker crusts

Preheat oven to 375° F.

In a large bowl, mix sugar, flour, spice, and salt. Stir in pumpkin, milk and egg.

Divide the mixture between the two pie crusts. If you are using a pastry crust, cut a strip of tin foil about 1½ inch wide and use it to cover the edge of the piecrust to prevent overbrowning. Place a cookie sheet in the oven. Place the pies on the cookie sheet and bake for 45 minutes, or until a knife inserted two inches from the edge comes out clean.

Makes 2 pies. Serve hot or cold with whipped topping.

No-Pecan Pie

1 unbaked pie crust, or one graham cracker crust
½ cup butter or margarine
1½ cups sugar
1 tablespoon vinegar
3 eggs
1 teaspoon vanilla extract
Pinch of salt

Preheat oven to 325° F.

In a saucepan, melt the butter. Stir in sugar and vinegar, and bring to a boil.

In a mixing bowl, beat the eggs thoroughly. Slowly add the hot liquid mixture to the eggs, beating well as you pour. Stir in vanilla and salt.

Pour the filling into the prepared crust. If you are using a pastry crust, cut a strip of tin foil about 1½ inch wide and cover the edge of the piecrust to prevent overbrowning. Bake for 60 minutes* or until the crust is golden brown and the filling is set.

• - If you wish, place pecans on top of the filling halfway through the baking process — but then it won't be *No*-Pecan Pie, will it?!

Currant Pudding

1 cup flour
¾ cup shortening
1 cup bread crumbs
¼ cup sugar
1 cup (5 oz.) dried currants
1 teaspoon baking powder
Pinch of salt

Grease a pudding mold (a stainless steel mixing bowl will do) and set aside.

In a large mixing bowl, sift together the flour, salt and baking powder. Add the shortening and cut it in with a pastry cutter or two knives until the mixture is crumbly. Stir in the bread crumbs, sugar and currants. Mix to form a stiff dough, adding small amounts of water if necessary to keep the dough workable.

Put the dough in the prepared pudding mold. Cover the mold with aluminum foil, and tie a length of string securely around the rim to hold the foil in place.

Prepare a steamer: Place a trivet inside a large pot — large enough to easily contain the greased bowl or pudding mold. An inverted disposable aluminum pie pan, with holes punched in it, will work as a trivet.

Place the mold on the trivet inside the large pot, and pour boiling water into the pot until the level of the water is halfway up the sides of the pudding mold. Cover the pot and simmer for 1½ hours.

Remove the pudding mold from the steamer. Carefully remove the aluminum foil, and turn the pudding out onto a serving plate.

Serve with *Custard Sauce* (also found in this cookbook).

Baklava

A famous treat from the Middle East!

PASTRY:
16 oz. frozen filo dough
  (21 16x12-inch sheets)
1½ cups butter or margarine,
  melted

FILLING:
4 cups finely chopped nuts
¼ cup sugar
2 teaspoons ground cinnamon
⅛ teaspoon ground cloves
2 teaspoons vanilla extract

SYRUP:
¾ cup sugar
¾ cup water
¾ cup honey
3 inches stick cinnamon
3 whole cloves
1 tablespoon lemon juice

Thaw frozen filo dough at room temperature for 2 hours. Cut the 16x12-inch sheets in half (8x12 inches; or, if the filo dough is a different size, cut to fit pan.) Cover with a slightly damp towel.

Lightly butter the bottom of a 13x9-inch baking pan. Layer nine of the half-sheets of filo in the pan, brushing each sheet with some of the melted butter. Mix together the walnuts, ¼ cup sugar, ground cinnamon, and vanilla extract. Sprinkle 1 cup of this mixture over the filo in the pan, and drizzle with some melted butter. Add four half-sheets of the filo, brushing each with more of melted butter.

Repeat the layers of nuts, melted butter and filo sheets 5 more times, brushing each sheet of filo with melted butter (margarine). Sprinkle the remaining nut mixture over the top, and drizzle with more of the melted butter (margarine). Place the remaining nine half-sheets of filo on top of the nut mixture, brushing each with the remaining melted butter (margarine).

Gently but firmly, cut diamond-shaped pieces or squares into the layers, cutting to *but not through* the bottom layer.

Bake in a 325° oven (300° F. if using a glass pan) for 50 minutes. Remove from oven, and re-cut the diamonds or squares all the way through. Allow to cool thoroughly.

In a small saucepan combine the ¾ cup sugar, water, honey, lemon juice, cloves, and stick cinnamon. Boil gently, uncovered, for 15 minutes. Remove from heat, and remove cloves and stick cinnamon. Stir the syrup until it is well blended, then pour over the cooled pastry.

Let cool completely. Garnish each diamond with a whole clove if desired. Delicious any way it's served!

Chocolate Baklava

To make a chocolate version of this already-decadent dessert, substitute the filling and add a glaze, as follows:

FILLING:
4 cup pecans or other nuts, finely chopped
2 teaspoons ground cinnamon
¼ cup sugar
1 cup (6 oz.) semi-sweet chocolate chips, melted

Follow the same directions for making Baklava, except pour the hot syrup over the pastry as soon as it comes out of the oven, then let the Baklava cool at least 4 hours.

Drizzle the Baklava with this glaze:

⅓ cup semi-sweet chocolate chips
1 tablespoon butter or margarine
1 tablespoon water

Combine the chocolate, butter, and water in a small pan or in a microwave dish. Heat over very low heat (or in the microwave) until the glaze is melted and smooth when stirred. Drizzle over the top and allow to cool until the glaze is firm.

Kadiyif

A simpler variation of Middle Eastern flavors

PASTRY:

6 large biscuits of
   shredded wheat cereal
½ cup milk
½ cup butter or margarine, melted

FILLING:

2 cups finely chopped nuts
2 tablespoons sugar
1 teaspoon ground cinnamon
A dash of ground cloves
1 teaspoon vanilla extract

SYRUP:

½ cup sugar
½ cup water
½ cup honey
3 inches stick cinnamon
3 whole cloves
2½ teaspoons lemon juice

Break the shredded wheat up in a bowl and pour milk over it. Allow the shredded wheat to soak for about 10 minute. Squeeze out and discard the milk.

Preheat oven to 375° F. (350° F. if using a glass pan). Butter an 8x8 -inch square baking dish and set aside.

In a small bowl, combine the walnuts, 2 tablespoons of sugar, ground cinnamon, and vanilla extract. Mix well and set aside.

Spread half of the soaked shredded wheat biscuits evenly in the bottom of the prepared baking dish, and brush with butter. Spread the nut filling evenly over the shredded wheat. Cover the filling evenly with the remaining shredded wheat. Brush with the remaining butter (margarine). Bake 45 minutes or until golden.

While the kadiyif is baking, prepare the syrup: In a saucepan, combine ½ cup of sugar, ½ cup water, the honey, lemon juice, cloves, and stick cinnamon. Boil gently, uncovered, for 15 minutes. Remove from heat, and remove cloves and stick cinnamon. Stir to blend completely, and allow to cool.

When the kadiyif is baked, remove it from the oven and pour the cooled syrup over it. Allow the entire dessert to cool and cut it into small squares to serve.

NOTE: If you are fortunate enough to have a Middle Eastern grocery store in your area, you can substitute ½ lb. of Kadiyif dough for the shredded wheat; do *not* soak it in milk.

Popcorn Balls

A favorite childhood treat

⅔ cup corn syrup or molasses
½ teaspoon salt
⅔ cup sugar
2 quarts popped popcorn, unbuttered
Food coloring, if desired

Pop the popcorn in your favorite fashion, and set aside.

In a saucepan, add the syrup, sugar, and salt, and bring to a boil over medium heat. Boil for 2 minutes, stirring constantly. If you wish to make the finished popcorn balls more festive, add food coloring.

Place popped popcorn in a large bowl and gradually pour syrup mixture over popcorn. Stir well with a spoon until all popcorn kernels are coated.

Allow the coated popcorn to cool enough to be safely handled. Butter your hands and, working quickly, shape the popcorn mixture into baseball-sized clumps.

Peanut Brittle

1 cup sugar
½ cup water
¼ cup light corn syrup
1 cup peanuts
¼ teaspoon salt
½ teaspoon butter or
  margarine
⅛ teaspoon baking soda

Grease a large baking sheet and set aside.

In a skillet or heavy saucepan, combine sugar, water and corn syrup. Cook at medium heat, stirring occasionally, until syrup turns golden brown (238° F. on a candy thermometer — soft ball stage.)

Stir in raw peanuts and salt. Continue stirring until mixture turns medium brown (290° F.* — soft crack stage.)

Remove from heat. Vigorously stir in margarine and baking soda. Pour out onto prepared baking sheet and let cool. Break into pieces.

Makes about 1 pound.

* - If you do not have a candy thermometer, test the candy by dropping a small amount into a cup of very cold water. At 'soft ball' stage, the candy will form a soft, squishable ball. At 'soft crack' stage, the mixture will separate into hard threads that will bend and not be brittle when removed from the water.

Cheesecake

This classic temptation can't be topped!

(Unless you have sweetened cherries, or blueberries, or strawberries, or chocolate...!)

1 pound cream cheese (two 8-oz. packages), softened
6 tablespoons sugar
1 large egg, lightly beaten
½ teaspoon vanilla extract
1 tablespoon cornstarch
½ cup sour cream

Preheat the oven to 400° F. (375° F. if you are using a glass pan.)

Place the cream cheese and sugar in a large glass or metal mixing bowl; beat them together until the mixture is smooth and light. Add eggs, vanilla, and cornstarch, and beat only until thoroughly mixed; be careful not to over-mix. Add the sour cream and gently stir until the mixture is well blended.

Pour the mixture into an ungreased 8-inch square or round baking pan. Bake for about 25-30 minutes.

Allow the cake to cool in the oven, with the door propped slightly open, for 3 hours.

Chill thoroughly before serving. Fabulous any way you serve it!

Bread Pudding

Whoever thought day-old bread could be so good?

2 slightly beaten eggs
2¼ cups milk
1 teaspoon vanilla extract
½ teaspoon ground cinnamon
¼ teaspoon salt
4 cups 1-inch cubes day-old bread
½ cup brown sugar
½ cup raisins (optional)

Preheat oven to 350°. Lightly grease an 8x8-inch baking pan and set aside.

In a mixing bowl, combine eggs, milk, vanilla, cinnamon, and salt. Stir in the bread cubes, then stir in the brown sugar and raisins. Pour the mixture into the prepared pan.

Place the pan inside a larger shallow pan (like a 9x13-inch rectangular pan), and place both in the oven. Pour hot water into the larger pan until it reaches about 1 inch up the sides of the smaller pan.

Bake for 45 minutes, or until a knife inserted halfway between the center and the edge comes out clean.

Makes 6-8 servings. Best served warm with cream and/or honey, but also delicious served by itself. Not bad cold, either!

Lemon Freeze

A cold and tangy treat

2 teaspoons grated lemon zest*
¾ cup fresh lemon juice
1 cup milk
1 cup cream or evaporated milk
1 cup sugar

In a large freezer-safe bowl, combine the lemon zest, lemon juice, milk, and cream. Add sugar and stir until the sugar is dissolved. Cover the bowl with plastic wrap and freeze 8 hours or overnight.

Remove Lemon Freeze from freezer. Puree mixture in a food processor, or beat with an electric mixer until smooth. Do not overbeat — the mixture should stay firm. Spoon into serving dish or dishes and freeze again until firm, about 2 hours.

Makes 6-8 servings.

* - No, lemon zest is not a soap; it is finely-grated peel from fresh lemons. Lemon zest can be stored frozen, and is a wonderful addition for many desserts!

Italian Ice

ORANGE ICE:

2 large oranges, peeled and seeded,
    with white membranes removed
½ cup frozen orange juice concentrate, thawed
1 cup water
1 packet unflavored gelatin
1 cup sugar (or to taste)
⅓ cup lemon juice

In a blender or food processor, puree the orange pulp. Combine with the orange concentrate in a mixing bowl and set aside.

In a saucepan, soften the gelatin in the water. Bring to a boil over medium heat. Add sugar, and stir until dissolved.

Pour the sugar/gelatin mixture into the orange mixture and add the lemon juice. Stir to blend. Pour into a shallow baking dish and freeze solid — at least 6 hours.

Remove the dish from the freezer and allow the ice to thaw slightly, until it is soft enough to cut with a knife. Cut the softened ice into cubes.

Place the cubes in a food processor or electric blender, and puree the cubes into a smooth, creamy slush.

Serve immediately, or refreeze in airtight containers. To serve the dessert after freezing, all to thaw for 15 minutes before serving.

Italian Ice works well with many fruits and flavors. Fresh fruit works best, but frozen fruit may also be used, adding a little extra sugar and lemon juice if needed to compensate for the lack of fresh fruit flavor. With seeded fruits (e.g. raspberries, blackberries), you can pulp and strain the fruit for a smoother ice.

Some easy variations include:

STRAWBERRY ICE:
Substitute 1 pint of hulled strawberries, pureed, for the orange pulp; omit the orange juice concentrate.

MELON ICE:
Substitute the pulp of 1 large canteloupe, pureed, for the orange pulp; omit the orange juice concentrate.

Banbury Cakes

These were once forbidden for being "sinfully rich!"

FILLING:

2 cups dried currants,
  rinsed and drained

1 cup sugar

1 teaspoon ground cinnamon

½ teaspoon ground nutmeg

¼ cup melted butter or
  margarine

PASTRY:

3 cups flour

2 tablespoons sugar

1½ teaspoons salt

1¼ cups shortening

7-9 tablespoons cold water

GLAZE:

1 egg white

1 tablespoon water

2 tablespoons sugar

In a medium-sized mixing bowl, combine all the filling ingredients. Mix well and set aside.

Prepare the pastry by combining flour, salt, and sugar in a large bowl. Stir or sift together until evenly blended. Cut in shortening with a pastry blender or two knives until the mixture looks crumbly. Add cold water a little at a time, mixing lightly with a fork. Shape dough into a ball with your hands, and divide in half. Refrigerate second half of dough while you are working with the first half.

On a lightly floured board, roll out the half of dough with a lightly floured rolling pin until the dough is about ⅛-inch thick. Cut into 2½-inch rounds with a cookie cutter. Place about a tablespoon of filling on half of the circles, leaving about ½-inch of dough around the edges. Flatten out the filling slightly. Moisten edges of dough with water. Place a second circle of dough over the top and seal the edges. Using a floured spatula, place the cakes on an ungreased cookie sheet and cut several slits across the top with a sharp knife.

When you are ready to bake your Banbury cakes, prepare the glaze: in a small bowl, combine the egg white and water. Using a pastry brush, brush this mixture over the tops of the cakes. Sprinkle with the sugar.

Bake at 450° F. for 12-15 minutes. Remove from baking sheets immediately and cool on cake racks. Continue the process and make the rest of the Banbury Cakes from the dough you have refrigerated.

Enjoy your "sinfully rich" Banbury Cakes warm or cold!

Eccles Cakes

A delicious variation on Banbury Cakes

To make Eccles Cakes, follow the same procedure used to make *Banbury Cakes* but replace the filling with the following:

FILLING:

3 tablespoons butter or margarine
½ cup brown sugar, packed into cup
½ cup raisins
¼ cup dried currants
¼ cup chopped candied peel
½ teaspoon ground allspice
¼ teaspoon ground cinnamon
¼ teaspoon ground nutmeg

Heat the butter and brown sugar in a medium saucepan over low heat. When butter (margarine) is melted, remove from heat. Add raisins, currants, chopped candied peel, and spices; mix all ingredients well and let cool.

Sweet Pilau

An East Indian version of rice pudding.

2 tablespoons butter or margarine
1½ cups cooked rice
   (or ¾ cups uncooked rice)
1½ cups milk
2 tablespoons sugar
⅛ teaspoon ground mace
1 teaspoon ground cinnamon
¼ teaspoon salt
¼ cup seedless raisins
¼ cup sliced blanched almonds

In a saucepan, melt the butter.

In a separate pan, cook the rice to make 1½ cups of cooked rice. (Instant rice works fine for this recipe.)

Add the cooked rice to the butter and stir until well combined.

Add the remaining ingredients and mix thoroughly. Bring to a boil and simmer, stirring frequently, until the rice has absorbed the milk and the mixture is thick; this should take about 10 to 15 minutes. Remove from heat and allow to cool slightly before serving.

Delicious served hot or cold!

Halva

More sweets from India!

2 cups water
1 cup sugar
1 cup (2 sticks) butter or margarine
1½ cups uncooked farina (like *Cream of Wheat*)
½ teaspoon ground cardamom
1 teaspoon ground cinnamon
¼ cup flaked coconut
⅔ cup coarsely chopped blanched almonds
⅔ cup raisins (optional)

Grease an 8-inch square pan and set aside.

In a small saucepan, combine the water and sugar. Boil for 10 minutes, or until a thin syrup forms.

In a larger saucepan, melt the butter. Add the farina and cook over low heat, stirring frequently, until the farina is very lightly browned. Add spices, coconut, almonds, raisins, and the hot sugar syrup; blend thoroughly. While still warm, press the mixture into the prepared pan in an even layer.

Cool at room temperature until set.

Cut into 2-inch squares and chill. Makes 16 squares.

Figgy Pudding

"We won't go until we get some!" (traditional)
"Won't go!! Won't go!!" (Animal, the Muppets)

¼ cup butter or margarine, softened
½ cup sugar
3 eggs
1 cup any combination of chopped figs, raisins, currants, or chopped dates
½ cup chopped pecans or other nuts
Flour
1 cup bread crumbs
1 teaspoon ground cinnamon
¼ teaspoon ground cloves
¼ teaspoon ground allspice

Preheat oven to 375° F. (350° F. if you are using a glass pan). Grease an 8-inch baking pan or casserole dish and set aside.

In a large mixing bowl, beat the butter until soft; gradually add the sugar and beat the combination until the mixture is creamy. Add the eggs one at a time, beating each thoroughly.

In a separate bowl, combine the figs and nuts. Sprinkle lightly with flour, and stir until the figs and nuts are lightly coated with the flour. Add this fig/nut mixture to the butter (margarine) mixture.

In another bowl, combine the bread crumbs and spices. Stir these ingredients into the butter mixture.

Turn the mixture into prepared pan and bake for ½ hour.

Delicious served with *Hard Sauce* (also found in this cookbook)!

Drinks

Strawberry Lemonade

1 pint fresh strawberries, cleaned and hulled
1½ cups cold water
6 tablespoons lemon juice
6 tablespoons to ½ cup sugar
1 cup chilled club soda

Use a blender to puree the strawberries. In a 1-quart pitcher, combine the pureed strawberries, water, lemon juice, and sugar. Stir briskly until the sugar dissolves. Add club soda.

Makes about 1 quart. Serve over ice and garnish as desired.

Quickie Version: substitute 1 cup strawberry daiquiri mixer for the fresh strawberries, and reduce sugar to ¼ cup.

Fresh-Squeezed Lemonade

¾ cup sugar
¼ cup boiling water
¾ cup fresh squeezed lemon juice (about 12 lemons)
1½ teaspoons grated lemon rind
2½ cups cold water
Lemon or lime slices
Fresh mint sprigs

In a large pitcher, combine sugar and boiling water. Stir until the sugar dissolves. This will make a strong, syrupy mix. Add the lemon rind, lemon juice, and cold water. Mix well and chill.

To serve, fill 8-12 oz. drinking glasses with ice. Pour the cold lemonade mix over the ice, filling the glass. Garnish with lemon or lime slices and fresh mint sprigs, if you wish.

Very refreshing!

Eggnog

This old-fashioned beverage is too good to be reserved only for the holidays!

½ cup pasteurized egg product (like EggBeaters)
2 to 4 tablespoons sugar
1 can (13 oz.) evaporated milk
¾ cup milk
1 teaspoon vanilla flavoring
1 teaspoon rum flavoring
Nutmeg (optional)

Place egg substitute and sugar in a pitcher and blend thoroughly using an electric beater or wire whisk. Mix in the evaporated milk, milk, vanilla extract, and rum flavoring.

Chill the eggnog overnight to enhance the flavor.

Pour into chilled mugs or glasses to serve. If you wish, top with a sprinkle of nutmeg.

Makes 3 cups.

Classi Lassi

A light, exotic flavor.

½ cup plain yogurt or buttermilk
1 cup water
2 cups crushed ice
1½ tablespoons sugar or honey
¼ teaspoon rosewater

Place the yogurt in a small bowl and stir until smooth. Add the water a little at a time, mixing well after each addition. Stir in the (sugar or honey) and rosewater.

Fill two 16-ounce drinking glasses with 1 cup each of crushed ice. Divide the yogurt mixture between each glass, pouring mixture over the ice, and serve.

Chocolate Soda

Nostalgic memories

2 tablespoons chocolate syrup
1 teaspoon milk
½ cup club soda
2 tablespoons of your favorite vanilla
   or chocolate-flavored frozen dessert
   (ice cream, ice milk, or frozen yogurt)

Place chocolate syrup in a 10-ounce glass. Add milk and ¼ cup club soda. Stir. Add ice cream. Add remaining ¼ cup club soda.
   Makes 1 fabulous serving.

Orange Soda

¼ cup orange juice
1 teaspoon lemon juice
1 tablespoon sugar
1 teaspoon milk.
½ cup club soda or your favorite lemon-lime soda pop
2 tablespoons of your favorite vanilla-flavored
   frozen dessert (ice cream, ice milk, or frozen yogurt)

Place orange juice, lemon juice, sugar, and milk in a 10-ounce glass. Add ¼ cup of the lemon-lime pop or club soda and the ice cream. Add remaining soda pop.
Makes 1 serving.

Egg Creams

¼ cup chocolate syrup
¼ cup evaporated milk or light cream
½ cup club soda (be sure the club soda is fresh and fizzy!)

Place syrup and cream in a tall glass and stir to blend. Slowly pour in club soda, stirring constantly.
Makes 1 serving — but serve immediately!

Quick Iced Latte

1 to 2 teaspoons instant coffee
2 teaspoons sugar, or to taste
1 tablespoon water
4 ice cubes
1 cup milk

Combine instant coffee, sugar, water, and ice cubes in a jar with a tight-fitting lid. Shake vigorously until the mixture is foamy, about 30 seconds. Remove the lid and add milk. Shake just enough to blend in the milk.
Makes 1 serving.

Hot Spiced Lemonade

Soothing sipping for a chilly evening.

½ cup lemon juice
3½ cups water
⅓ cup honey
1 3-inch stick cinnamon
8 whole cloves

Place all ingredients in a saucepan and mix well. Heat to simmer, taking care that it does not boil over. Simmer gently for about 20 minutes to blend the spices.
Serve hot, sit back and enjoy!

Hot Mulled Cider

Chases away winter chills

8 SERVINGS:
1 teaspoon whole allspice
1 teaspoon whole cloves
¼ teaspoon salt
A dash of ground nutmeg
3 inches stick cinnamon
2 quarts apple cider

2 SERVINGS:
¼ teaspoon whole allspice
¼ teaspoon whole cloves
A dash of salt
A dash of ground nutmeg
1½ inches stick cinnamon
2 cups apple cider

In a large saucepan combine all ingredients. Slowly bring to a boil, taking care that it does not boil over. Cover and simmer 20 minutes. Remove spices. Serve in warmed mugs.

SUBSTITUTION:
Cranberry juice or grape juice can be substituted for the apple cider.

Siberian Nights

A hot instant tea mix

2 cups presweetened orange breakfast drink mix
1 cup presweetened lemonade mix
1 cup instant tea
1 teaspoon ground cloves
2 teaspoons ground cinnamon

Put all ingredients into a mixing bowl and blend with a spoon or wire whisk. Store in a covered container.

To serve, mix 1 or 2 tablespoons in hot water or (according to taste).

SUBSTITUTION:
Omit the presweetened drink mixes. Instead, use 2 packets of unsweetened orange drink mix (enough to make 1 gallon of drink); 1 packet of unsweetened lemonade drink mix (enough for 2 quarts of drink); and 2 cups of sugar.

East Indian Tea

Serve this with your Halva and Nankhatai.

2½ cups water
2½ cups milk
3 teaspoons loose green tea*
1 teaspoon loose black tea*
1 teaspoon ground cardamom
½ teaspoon almond extract
3 inches stick cinnamon
2 whole cloves

In a large saucepan, combine all ingredients. Over low heat, heat to a simmer, taking care that the mixture does not boil over. Simmer gently for 15 to 20 minutes. Strain out spices and teas and pour into cups.

Makes about 5 servings. Sweeten to taste with sugar, honey or artificial sweetener.

* - If you wish, 3 teabags of green tea and 1 teabag of black tea can be used instead of loose tea.

Jazzy Coffee

To jazz up one cup of your favorite hot coffee, add:

½ teaspoon extract of your choice:
   Vanilla, Mint, Almond or Orange
Sugar or sweetener (to taste)
2 tablespoons cream, milk, or coffee creamer

Dissolve all ingredients in hot coffee.
Top the prepared coffee with:

2 heaping tablespoons frozen whipped topping
½ teaspoon chocolate sprinkles

Serve with a spoon and enjoy!

Cafe au Latte Mix

⅓ cup instant coffee
1 cup dry milk
2 tablespoons powdered coffee creamer
½ cup powdered sugar
¼ cup instant cocoa drink (optional)

In a mixing bowl, combine all ingredients using a spoon or wire whisk. Add the instant cocoa mix if you wish a mocha-flavored drink.

Store the dry mixture in a tightly covered container.

To serve, use one or two heaping teaspoonfuls of the latte mix per cup of boiling water.

Cocoa Mix

2 cups non-fat dry milk powder
¾ cup sugar
½ cup unsweetened cocoa, sifted*
½ cup powdered non-dairy creamer
A dash of salt

In large mixing bowl, combine all ingredients using a spoon or a wire whisk. Store in tightly covered container.

This recipe makes about 3¾ cups of dry mix, which will make about 15 6-ounce servings of cocoa.

When you're ready for that cup of cocoa, combine ¼ cup of cocoa mix with ¾ cup of boiling water in a mug. Stir to blend.

*Use "Dutch" (European) Style cocoa for a smoother chocolate flavor.

Fiesta Hot Chocolate

Enjoy a Southwestern flair

3 tablespoons unsweetened cocoa, sifted	A dash of ground cloves
2 tablespoons honey	Pinch of salt
¼ cup hot water	1 teaspoon instant coffee
A dash of ground cinnamon	2 cups milk
	Marshmallows for topping

Place all ingredients (except milk and marshmallows) in a small saucepan. Stir over medium heat until the mixture reaches the boiling point. Turn down heat. Keep stirring and allow the mixture to simmer for 30 seconds, then stir in the milk. Continue heating until the mixture is hot, but do not let it boil. Pour into mugs and top with the marshmallows. Add an extra sprinkling of cinnamon, if you like.

Makes 2 friendly servings — an invitation to share!

Fillings, Frostings and Other Toppings

Chocolate Frosting

1½ cups powdered sugar
6 tablespoons unsweetened cocoa, sifted
A dash of salt
3 tablespoons milk
1 teaspoon vanilla
3 tablespoons butter or margarine, softened

Using a sifter, mix together the powdered sugar, cocoa and salt into a large mixing bowl. (Sifting removes any lumps in the powdered sugar and cocoa.)

Add milk and vanilla. Beat until smooth, using a spoon or an electric mixer. Add the butter and continue beating until the frosting is smooth and easy to spread.

This recipe makes about 1 cup of frosting—more than enough for an 8x8-inch square cake. Double the recipe if you wish to make enough frosting for a 2-layer cake.

Generic Frosting

2 tablespoons shortening, softened
¼ teaspoon salt
1 teaspoon vanilla extract
2 tablespoons milk
1½ cups powdered sugar, sifted

In a small mixing bowl, mix the shortening, salt, vanilla, and about ¾ cup of the powdered sugar, beating all together with a spoon or electric mixer. Alternate adding milk and the rest of the powdered sugar; mix each addition until smooth and creamy. (Add more powdered sugar if the frosting is too thin. If the frosting is too thick to spread, add a little more milk.)

Makes enough frosting to frost an 8-inch cake.

Double this recipe if you wish to make enough frosting for a 2-layer cake.

FROSTINGS OF DISTINCTION:
• You can make frostings of almost any flavor by substituting other extract flavorings for the vanilla extract in this recipe. Some flavorful suggestions include mint, lemon, almond, or rum.
• Add a few drops of food coloring to corresponds with the flavoring. For example, use green food coloring with mint flavoring, yellow food coloring with lemon flavoring, etc.

Cocoa Fluff

*A light, fluffy frosting
with the great taste of chocolate!*

1 envelope (1.3 oz.) dry whipped topping mix
½ cup cold skim milk
1 tablespoon unsweetened cocoa, sifted
½ teaspoon vanilla extract

   In a small mixing bowl, stir together the whipped topping mix, milk, cocoa and vanilla. Beat with an electric mixer on high speed for about 4 minutes or until the fluff forms soft peaks. Use immediately, or refrigerate until needed.

Hard Sauce

½ cup butter or margarine, softened
2 cups powdered sugar, sifted
2 teaspoons vanilla extract or 1 teaspoon brandy extract

   In a mixing bowl, cream butter (margarine) using a spoon or electric mixer. Gradually add sugar and vanilla. Cream thoroughly until very smooth. Store in refrigerator.

Cream Cheese Frosting

Excellent on carrot cake or other sweet desserts!

4 ounces cream cheese, softened
1 tablespoon milk
½ teaspoon vanilla extract
2 cups powdered sugar, sifted

   Put the cream cheese and milk in a small glass or metal bowl, and beat just until smooth. Gradually beat in the vanilla and powdered sugar.
   If the frosting is too thick for suitable spreading consistency, add a little more milk. If the frosting is too thin, add a little more powdered sugar.

Custard Sauce

A favorite addition to many British desserts

2½ cups milk
2 tablespoons cornstarch
3 egg yolks
1½ teaspoons brandy extract
¼ cup sugar

Measure 3 tablespoons of milk into a mixing bowl and stir in the cornstarch, egg yolks, brandy flavoring and sugar. Beat until smooth.

In a saucepan, bring the remaining milk just to a boil. Add the hot milk to the cornstarch mixture and mix thoroughly. Return the mixture to the saucepan and simmer briefly to thicken.

Perfect to top many of your favorite desserts.

Lemon Curd

A sweet and tangy spread for fresh-baked treats!

1 cup sugar
1 cup lemon juice (about 5 large lemons)
3 tablespoons firm margarine or butter, cut up
3 eggs or 6 egg yolks

Locate a clean 1-pint glass container. (A canning jar is perfect.) Have the jar ready at warm room temperature.

Mix the sugar and lemon juice in a heavy saucepan. Stir in the margarine and eggs. Cook over low heat or in a double boiler, stirring constantly with a spoon or wire whisk. Do not allow mixture to boil, and keep stirring at all times.

The mixture will thicken and coat the back of the spoon within 10-20 minutes. *Immediately* pour the hot curd through a strainer into the 1-pint container.

Cover and refrigerate. (Storage life: about 2 months.)

Afterword

So here we are at the end of *Sweet Treats*.

How did it all happen? Well --

Marsha and I have been sharing recipes for as long as I can remember, but they were always a sideline interest for me. Where Marsha was concerned, my creative efforts were to illustrate her many adventures; hers, and those of her friends, and *their* friends, and some folks she had never heard of, and some she would never ever meet....

A few years ago, my soulmate encouraged me to combine my love for cooking with my love for cartooning. Marsha picked outfits she felt were appropriate for recipes of various nationalities, and our Recipe Cards were born. To my delight they went over very well at the conventions where they appeared, and I kept on doing them.

After a couple of years we decided to put out a cookbook combining the more popular Recipe Cards with recipes I'd enjoyed putting together. It was going to be self-published and sold at conventions -- purely small-scale stuff.

Enter Darrell Benvenuto, who saw our Recipe Cards at a convention in California. He wrote to ask if we had ever thought about putting together a cookbook using the Recipe Card artwork... the result is what you're reading now!

There are a lot of people who deserve thanks for their support and encouragement. From our friend Phil Morrissey who originally got us to send artwork to conventions; to Darrell at MedSystems who decided to take a chance on the book; and to all our friends who expressed interest and enthusiasm... all deserve thanks and appreciation!

Most of all, I want to thank my wonderful soulmate, a loving and multi-talented person in his own right, who bravely put up with the endless experiments which culminated in this book. All the recipes herein are successes; but there were failures along the way, and some of them were spectacular. He survived and stayed supportive, and that's about as amazing and wonderful as it gets!

Finally: thanks to you for buying this book. I hope you find it fun and useful for many years to come.

— *Margaret Carspecken*

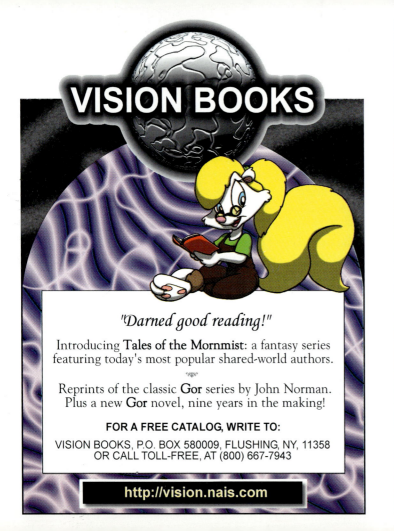
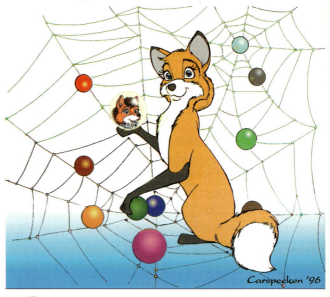